HARRY S TRUMAN
A PICTORIAL BIOGRAPHY

HARRY S
TRUMAN

A PICTORIAL BIOGRAPHY

By JOSEPH GIES

1968

DOUBLEDAY & COMPANY, INC.

Garden City, New York

Library of Congress Catalog Card Number 67–19087
Copyright © 1968 by Doubleday & Company, Inc.
All Rights Reserved
Printed in the United States of America
First Edition

CONTENTS

LIST OF PHOTOGRAPHS

PHOTO CREDITS

Photographs from the following agencies appear on pages listed below:

Acme Newspictures, 37, 50, 65, 85, 93, 101, 107, 111, 123, and 147

Associated Press, 30

Brown Brothers, 6, 7, 11, 18, 31, 36, 50, 58, 59, 71, 80, 87, 100, 106, 119, 156, and 157

European Picture Service, 3

Ford News Bureau, 85

Fred Ward from Black Star, 70

Harris and Ewing News Photos, 49, and 59

International News Photo, 86, 107, 119, 137, and 140

Los Alamos Scientific Laboratory, 70

Olie Atkins of Saturday Evening Post, 122

Tass from Sovfoto, 55, 75, and 91

United States Air Force, 70

U. S. Army, 55, and 147

United Press International, 3, 6, 7, 10, 30, 37, 41, 44, 51, 65. 74, 75, 77, 80, 81, 90, 93, 101, 110, 120, 121, 123, 129, 130, 131, 136, 146, 153, 156, 157, 160, and 161

United Nations, 60, and 141

United Press Association, 27

Washington Post, 110

Wide World Photos, 3, 10, 11, 18, 19, 23, 27, 40, 43, 64, 81, 87, 90, 91, 100, 112, 117, 119, 122, 129, 130, 133, 140, 151, 160, 161, and 167

Zionist Archives and Library, 92

HARRY S TRUMAN

A PICTORIAL BIOGRAPHY

1884–1922

A MISSOURI BOY GROWS UP

Harry S Truman was born in Lamar, Missouri, on May 8, 1884, into an America of farms and small towns, horses, and mules. His father, John Anderson Truman, was a farmer and a horse trader, a small, tough, wiry man, quick with his words and handy with his fists. Once when he was a witness in a court case an overbearing lawyer as good as called him a liar. John Truman jumped out of the witness chair and chased the lawyer all the way out of the courthouse.

Harry's mother, Martha Young Truman, was a pioneer woman with an intellectual bent toward books and music, and prejudice against Yankees— they had robbed her family's farm during the Civil War. Along with his younger brother Vivian and his baby sister Mary Jane, Harry grew up on the huge Young farm—six hundred acres—near Grandview, in Jackson County, in western Missouri. He rode a Shetland pony with a saddle so beautifully made that sixty-five years later Vivian had it restored for a grandchild. He learned all about farming, from milking cows to making hay. In late summer he watched the threshing machine, worked by horses on a treadmill, and in the fall the hog-killing. The lard was rendered in a giant iron kettle that dated from before the War (it must have been too heavy for the Yankees to steal). One of his earliest memories was a shining one of his Grandfather Young taking him to the Belton Fair in the two-wheeled cart. They sat in the grandstand and watched the races, eating striped candy and peanuts.

In 1890 John Anderson Truman moved his family to Independence, into a big house on South Chrisler Street, with several acres of yard, big barns with horses and ponies, and chicken houses. Martha Truman took the three children to the nearest Protestant Sunday school, which happened to be the First Presbyterian, at Lexington and Pleasant Streets. In the fall of 1892 Harry started public school. He could already read, having benefited from his mother's head-start program. When it turned out that he had poor eyesight, she got him glasses, not too common an advantage in the 1890s.

The doctor somewhat overimpressed mother and son with the danger of breaking the glasses, and as a result Harry had to forego most of the rough-and-tumble games of the playground. He spent the extra time in the library where he developed a fondness for history books, and in practicing the piano. His mother gave him his first lessons and it was apparent that he had inherited her musical talent. But horses and ponies provided plenty of outdoor activity. Harry and Vivian also had fun with a little wagon to which they hitched a team of red goats.

When he was ten Harry suffered a severe attack of diphtheria. For a time he was actually paralyzed, and had to be carried from room to room. It was weeks before he recovered completely. As he slowly convalesced, he played with the doctor's son, a boy who shared some of his interests, and together they constructed a replica of the timber bridge Julius Caesar's Roman legionaries built across the Rhine.

In 1896, when he was twelve, the family moved to another big house, at 909 West Waldo Avenue. Harry, who had had chores to do since he was old enough to toddle, acquired a new one—driving two or three cows and calves to pasture a mile outside town and bringing them back in the evening. He and Vivian shared another country boy's task, splitting wood for the stove. The new barn had a hayloft where Harry, Vivian, and their friends planned Tom Sawyer adventures. There was a dovecote too, where they raised pigeons.

At school Harry was a favorite with teachers, many of whom he remembered affectionately fifty years later. His preferred study continued to be history, which he devoured—ancient, European, and American. It was the history of nineteenth-century historians, personal, anecdotal, heavily military and political, and full of lessons. He always believed his history reading stood him in good stead in the presidency, and perhaps it did, though by modern historians' standards, the picture of the world it gave him tended to be undercomplicated and moralistic.

When he was thirteen his proficiency on the piano had outrun Martha

John Anderson Truman and Martha Young Truman posed for this photo on their wedding day, December 28, 1881. John Truman was a farmer and horse trader, Martha an "unreconstructed Rebel" who instilled in her son Harry a love of music and books.

Future President, age six months, in Lamar, Missouri, late 1884.

The Truman brothers. Vivian, seated, was two years younger. Their costumes, including Harry's cane, were typical of fashionable children's portraits of the 1880s.

Truman's teaching, so she started him on regular lessons. His teacher was a student of the Viennese professor who taught Paderewski and Rubinstein, and she made Harry Truman the best musician who ever became President of the United States.

Before he was out of high school he took on his first "paying job," opening up Jim Clinton's drugstore at 6:30 A.M., mopping the floor, sweeping the sidewalk and cleaning the medicine bottles, the last an open-end task that kept him occupied till schooltime. Behind the prescription case stood the whiskey. There were plenty of saloons around the square in Independence, but church members and Anti-Saloon Leaguers did not like to be seen in them. Instead, they dropped into Jim Clinton's first thing in the morning and took an eye-opener back of the prescription case at ten cents a shot. The observation "gave a fourteen-year-old boy quite a viewpoint on the public front of leading citizens and 'amen-corner-praying' churchmen," he recalled later. His first week's wages were three silver dollars, which he tried to give his father.

In 1900, when he was sixteen, the Democratic National Convention was held in Kansas City. John Truman, a Democratic party hanger-on, sat through every session, and took Harry to several. The convention was dominated by William Jennings Bryan, the hero of the Western farmers, and Harry picked up a taste for grass roots liberalism and the fight of the common man against the power of great wealth.

The next year Harry graduated from Independence High School, where he had distinguished himself in his studies and had helped found a new school magazine, *Gleam,* which is still published today. Among his classmates were his closest friend, Charlie Ross, and a pretty golden-haired, blue-eyed girl named Bess Wallace, with whom he had been secretly in love since the fifth grade.

He had hopes of an appointment to West Point or Annapolis, and had done extra studying in algebra and Latin, but the Army recruiting station in Kansas City told him his eyesight would disqualify him. His chances of going to an ordinary college were knocked out by a piece of bad luck on his father's part. John Truman had progressed from livestock trading to real estate and finally speculation in grain futures; one bad guess suddenly wiped out his growing capital, and he was reduced to taking a job as a watchman. Harry got a job as timekeeper with a work gang on the Santa Fe Railroad. He kept track of the hours put in by the hoboes—migrant railroad workers who camped on the job—and paid them off, $1.50 for every ten-hour working day. The payoff was made Saturday night in a saloon in either Independence or Sheffield, the idea being that if the men could spend all their money on the spot they would show up for work again on Monday. Harry Truman's salary was $35 a month and board, with "a very down-to-earth education in the handling of men" thrown in.

The contract was finished in the spring of 1902. Before looking for another job Harry went on a trip with his father to inspect some land John Truman had bought in southern Missouri. They took the buggy and team, and had to ford the flooded Eleven Point River thirteen times, with the water coming up to the floorboards. The land turned out not to be worth much, and John Truman decided to return to the Grandview farm. Harry and his brother Vivian got jobs as clerks in a Kansas City bank, moving into a boardinghouse where a fellow boarder was Arthur Eisenhower, who had a brother named Dwight. "Harry and I had only a dollar a week left over from our board and room for riotous living," Arthur recalled later. Nevertheless, Harry managed to catch "every vaudeville show that came to the old Orpheum and the Grand."

He was good at the banking business, and got fast promotions. His salary of thirty-five dollars a month became sixty, and within five years a hundred twenty-five, princely for a young man of 1904. He uncovered a natural talent for getting along with people. Every so often he brought the chief clerk, head bookkeeper and paying teller out to the Grandview farm for a chicken dinner—"My mother was great on fried chicken, baked ham, hot biscuits and custard pie."

John Truman was helping his brother-in-law Harrison Young run the big Grandview farm. When Harrison Young decided to retire, John, who also had a job as road overseer of Jackson County, asked Harry to come out and take over. A few years later John Truman died following an operation, but by then Harry had proved himself to be as good a dirt farmer as he had been a bank clerk. The Grandview farm brought in $15,000 a year income, putting it far up in the top brackets of American farming. When Grandmother Young died in 1909 her estate was valued at $150,000, though most of the cash went for taxes and litigation over relatives' claims.

At Grandview Harry also got his feet wet in politics, serving as Democratic clerk on Election Day. He knew everybody in the precinct and was "kin" to most of them. Every election there was one Socialist vote cast.

Miss Ewing's first-grade class at Noland School, in Independence, Missouri. Harry, extreme left, bottom row, loved school and was a favorite of his teacher, standing in the doorway.

Glasses became a Truman trademark at the age of eight. They prevented him from going in for rough-and-tumble sports, and led to his spending maximum time in the library, where his favorite reading was history books.

A Missouri hayride. Blue-eyed, golden-haired Bess Wallace is seated, left, with Harry standing next to her aboard a wagon on the huge farm near Grandview that belonged to Truman's mother's family.

National Guardsman. Truman joined Battery B in Kansas City when it was organized in 1905, paying 25 cents a week for the privilege of drilling in the armory. When America entered World War I he was commissioned a lieutenant.

Once there were two. Judge Hall, a Republican, turned to Truman, puzzled, and asked, "Harry, it looks like old man Green has voted twice. Do you reckon he did?" Harry explained no, it was just that old man Green's son had reached voting age.

Before leaving Kansas City, Harry had joined the new National Guard outfit, Battery B, field artillery, and he kept up his drill, paying twenty-five cents a week for the privilege of using the armory. A cousin of his mother's introduced him to the Masonic lodge at Belton, Missouri. He became so enthusiastic a Mason that within three years he was master of his own newly founded Grandview Lodge.

As general manager and part owner of a large and successful farm enterprise Harry Truman presently found himself looking around for investment opportunities. In Kansas, Missouri, and Oklahoma test drilling was opening up oil fields for which the newly arrived automobile was creating a fabulous market. In 1916 Truman put five thousand dollars into a partnership with a Kansas City lawyer friend and an experienced oil man from Oklahoma. The company was later turned into a corporation with sixty thousand shares of stock and a large block of leases in Kansas. Only a sudden manpower shortage stopped it from drilling into what later turned out to be the Teter Oil Pool, one of the biggest in the mid-continent.

That manpower shortage resulted from America's entrance into the First World War, an event which had major impact in other ways on Harry Truman's career.

Though he modestly hoped for a promotion to section sergeant, no one was surprised when ex-National Guardsman Truman was commissioned a first lieutenant. After some training and drilling in Kansas City Convention Hall and on the streets, old Battery B, together with Battery C of Independence, greatly enlarged by new recruiting, became the 129th Field Artillery of the 35th Infantry Division, and in September entrained for Fort Sill, Oklahoma.

Thirty-three-year-old Harry Truman made a first-rate officer. Besides his regular duties he ran the regimental canteen. Picking a young enlisted man named Eddie Jacobson, who knew something about storekeeping, to help him, he collected two dollars per man from each battery for capital of $2200, stocked up the regimental store with cigarettes and stationery, sewed up the pockets of his enlisted clerks, and in six months paid back the $2200 plus $15,000 in dividends.

En route overseas, he took advantage of a twenty-four-hour pass to buy three new pairs of glasses, for which the patriotic optometrist refused payment.

In France he soon found himself in command of a battery—"Dizzy D," as it was known, from trouble it had given previous commanders. Captain Truman (his promotion was approved, but an Army foul-up delayed his notification for several months) called all the non-coms together and gave them some blunt information: "I didn't come over here to get along with you. You've got to get along with me. If there are any of you who can't, speak up right now and I'll bust you back right now." He observed, "We got along."

His technique in handling court-martial cases was simple. Rather than hold a formal court-martial, he sat back of a table, looked "as mean as I could," and told the culprit, "You can have a court-martial, or you can take what I give you." It worked fine. The Army was a school of practicality in human relations.

After learning to fire French 75s, supplied to American artillery outfits in a 1918 version of Lend-Lease, Captain Truman led his outfit into the line in the Vosges Mountains. The night after arrival came an episode known afterward as the Battle of Who Run. Ordered to fire a barrage of gas shells, the 129th unwittingly broke a silent agreement between the opposing lines and turned a quiet sector into a lively one. The German retaliatory fire caused a panic among the rookie artillerymen, who "scattered like partridges." Captain Truman finally got his battery back together without loss, though six horses were killed.

From then on, Battery D was a seasoned outfit. In September it supported 35th Division infantry in the offensive against the Saint-Mihiel salient, and in October moved with the division to the Argonne Forest for the biggest battle American soldiers had ever fought in. A number of years later a regimental runner named Paul Shaffer, who in civilian life had been a Kansas blacksmith, retained a vivid recollection of an action by the "Truman Battery."

". . . When they gave me the message that afternoon, it was for the Truman battery.

"I set out on the run, jumping into shell holes when I heard one with my name on it . . . I doubt any blacksmith ever ran so fast.

"I reached the battery in nothing flat, as muddy as an alligator, all the

Somewhere in France. Armed with three pairs of glasses, Captain Truman landed in France on April 13, 1918. Above, with three fellow officers of the "Truman Battery"—Battery D, 129th Field Artillery, 35th Division. Truman's later political career was largely founded on wartime associations.

The Argonne Forest. On the morning the major Allied offensive began the Truman Battery fired 3000 rounds from its French 75-mm guns between 4 A.M. and 8 A.M.

"Truman and Jacobson" men's furnishings store stood on Twelfth Street in downtown Kansas City, near the Muehlebach Hotel. At first the two veterans made money, but the depression of 1921–22 ruined business and shrank the value of their inventory, forcing them to close out at a heavy loss. Jacobson was finally compelled to go through bankruptcy, but Truman (left foreground) succeeded in holding out and eventually paying off all his debts.

Judge Truman. His steppingstone to the national political scene was the office of "judge," or county supervisor, of his native Jackson County, Missouri. His fight for good roads and buildings won him a reputation as an honest, energetic public servant who, as Boss Tom Pendergast perceived, made a strong candidate for the U. S. Senate in 1934.

skin off my nose. Captain Harry S Truman was standing there, his tin hat pushed on the back of his head, directing salvos into some spot toward the northeast. He was a banty officer in spectacles, and when he read my message he started runnin' and cussin' all at the same time, shouting for the guns to turn northwest. He ran about a hundred yards to a little knoll, and what he saw didn't need binoculars. I never heard a man cuss so well or so intelligently, and I'd shoed a million mules. He was shouting back ranges and giving bearings.

"The battery didn't say a word. They must have figured the cap'n could do the cussin' for the whole outfit. It was a great sight, like the center ring in Barnum and Bailey at the close of the show, everything clockwork, setting fuses, cutting fuses, slapping shells into breeches and jerking lanyards before the man hardly had time to bolt the door. Shell cases were flipping back like a jugglers' act, clanging on tin hats of the ammunition passers, the guns just spitting fire.

"Then Captain Truman ran down the knoll and cussed 'em to fire even faster. When he ran back up the hill still cussin', I forgot how I didn't want to get killed and I ran with him. I couldn't see our infantry. It must have been driven back to the little knoll, trying to crawl around and change front. Beyond it was some mighty fine grazing land, and at the far end a clump of woods, pretty leaves still on the autumn trees . . . Captain Truman had his binoculars on them. There were groups of Germans at the edge of the woods, stooping low and coming on slowly with machine guns on their hips . . .

"He shouted some cusswords filled with figures down to the battery, and shells started breaking into the enemy clumps . . . He really broke up that counterattack. He was still there being shot at when I came to my senses and got off the knoll.

"I went back to the sweating battery, but counterbatteries started ranging. They were looking for me and Captain Truman. I knew he had to move soon and I wished I could stay when he brought up the animals. Being from Topeka, I wanted to hear what a Missouri man had to say to his mules. But it wasn't a safe place for an out-of-work blacksmith. So I went back and told my major how Captain Truman and I had broken up a counterattack. I never saw the cussin' captain again until I voted for him in 1948."*

* From *The Doughboys* by Laurence Stallings.

On Armistice night a neighboring French battery, celebrating with a carload of wine sent up on the ammunition railway, came to pay respects to their allies, shouting, *"Vive Président Wilson!"* and *"Vive le capitaine d'artillerie américain!"*

Before sailing home, Captain Truman got a leave to visit Paris, where he enjoyed the opera—*Manon* and *Carmen*—but found the *Folies Bergère* "disgusting."

Back home in Independence, he finally married Bess Wallace, the girl he had been in love with since school days, and to whom he had become engaged before going overseas. Just why the courtship was so deliberate— bride and bridegroom were both thirty-five—is a mystery. The Wallaces may have been a cut above the Trumans socially and financially, but despite John Truman's unlucky grain speculation the family had remained solidly respectable and reasonably well off. Harry Truman may have been hoping to strike it rich in oil or some other business before asking the girl of his dreams to marry him.

After a honeymoon trip to Chicago and Port Huron, Michigan, the couple returned to Independence, settling in the big Wallace house on North Delaware.

Harry Truman had decided against going back to farming, and casting about for a business venture he hit on the idea of a partnership with Eddie Jacobson, the young man who had helped him make the regimental canteen a success. Raising $15,000 by selling off equipment and stock from the farm, he leased a site on Twelfth Street in downtown Kansas City, near the Muehlebach Hotel, and the Truman & Jacobson Haberdashery was opened. In their first year the two partners grossed $70,000. But in 1921 depression hit the country. Democrat Harry Truman blamed it then and afterward on the deflationary policies of Republican Secretary of the Treasury Andrew Mellon, who in seeking to "put labor in its place" sent farm prices to an all-time low and ruined small businessmen in the farm regions. Not only did sales hit bottom but dollar value of inventories dropped catastrophically. In 1922 the store had to close out, deeply in debt.

The experience gave Truman an insight not only into the problems of small businessmen, but into economics. Every good American is frightened to death of inflation, but not many are aware of the effects of deflation.

Both partners made strenuous efforts to avoid bankruptcy, and to pay off their debts in full. Jacobson, who got a job as a salesman, finally had to give up and declare himself bankrupt. Harry Truman was able to stave off bank-ruptcy and eventually pay every dollar of his debts. By the time he finished he was through with merchandising for good and embarked on an entirely different career.

FROM MISSOURI TO WASHINGTON

HARRY TRUMAN was a born-and-bred Democrat. His father had been a part-time member of the Kansas City Democratic organization, which was split into two factions, the Rabbits and the Goats. The Goats were led by Tom Pendergast, the beefy image of an old-fashioned American political boss, whose chief aide was his brother Mike. Mike's son Jim had been an officer in the 129th Field Artillery, and when in the spring of 1922 his father and uncle were looking for a strong candidate for county judge from the Eastern District of Jackson County, Jim suggested Harry Truman. With the haberdashery business failing Truman agreed to be available. At a meeting of township leaders Mike Pendergast described his candidate as a returned soldier, a captain "whose men didn't want to shoot him." Besides his exemplary war record, Truman's Masonic degrees were a political asset.

"County judge" in Missouri was actually the equivalent of county commissioner. A board of three judges levied taxes, built and repaired county roads, maintained homes for the aged and schools for delinquents, and administered other county functions. In Jackson County, Democratic nomination was tantamount to election, which made nomination a hotly contested prize. Truman found himself running against the Rabbit candidate, another candidate put up by the newly dissident Bulger faction, and two independents. Most of his rivals were political veterans, but newcomer Harry Truman demonstrated unmistakable aptitude for the game. Weighing down the rear end of his old Dodge roadster with two bags of cement he set out on the rough county roads. He shook hands and solicited votes in every township and precinct in the Eastern District, enlisting the support of wartime buddies, Masons, and the numerous Trumans, Youngs and Wallaces scattered through the county. On primary day he won a plurality of five hundred. Rabbit boss Joe Shannon, whose defeated candidate was a banker, commented sourly that the voters preferred "a busted merchant to a prosperous banker." Truman agreed: "Most people were broke, and they sympathized with a man in politics who admitted his financial condition."

The Shannon faction succeeded in electing the presiding judge of the three-man panel, but the other district judge was also a Goat, and as Truman candidly records, "we promptly took all the jobs." That was what the whole thing was about, from the viewpoint of the Pendergasts. But Judge Truman proved to be an intelligent, conscientious administrator, scrupulously honest. Out of his modest salary he continued to make payments on his haberdashery debts.

In 1924 the Shannon faction got even by throwing their support to Truman's Republican opponent in the November election. Truman suffered his first—and only—defeat. The Ku Klux Klan, which was experiencing a bizarre resurgence on a nationwide basis, also helped beat him. Someone introduced Truman to a Klan organizer, who tried to extract a promise that he would not give any jobs to Catholics. "I had a Catholic battery in the war," Truman told him, "and if any of those boys need help I'm going to give them a job."

The man who unseated Truman was an old harness-maker named Henry Rummel, who thirty years earlier had made an especially fine harness for the Truman boys' goat cart.

Temporarily Truman took a job recruiting for the Kansas City Automobile Club. He could not afford any lapse in income, because Bess had just presented him with a baby daughter. Born February 17, 1924, Margaret was the Trumans' only child.

Besides the auto club, Truman also got started in a profitable building-and-loan business. But he had been bitten by the political bug, and was eager to run for office again. Mike Pendergast thought he might try for county collector, a job that paid well, but Tom Pendergast had already promised that plum to someone else and suggested that Truman run instead for presiding judge.

One of the Pendergasts' political foes was widely blamed for the cheap, badly surfaced "pie-crust" roads with which the county was afflicted, and which Truman pledged himself to remedy. He expressed the conviction that "honest work for the county is the best politics." After easily winning nomination and election on that platform, he demonstrated that he had meant what he said. Journeying to Chicago and St. Louis to talk to bankers, he got the interest rate on tax-anticipation notes, used for county financing, cut from 6 percent to 4 percent, and later to 2½ percent. Then he got the Pendergasts to agree to let him propose a $6,500,000 bond issue. Neither the Pendergasts nor their implacable enemy the *Kansas City Star* believed the voters would approve the issue, but Truman persuaded them not only to vote this issue, but a little later a second one of $3,500,000 for more roads and $5,000,000 for a new courthouse in Independence. "I . . . told the taxpayers just how I would handle the bond money, and they believed me," he said. In doing so, Truman revealed a political secret weapon that would prove invaluable twenty years later: the gift of overt honesty. Listening to him argue for something, some voters might think the earnest, plain-spoken fellow in glasses was mistaken, but they would never figure he was lying.

One day Truman received a phone call from Tom Pendergast saying that some friends of his would like to talk to Truman about the contracts he was getting. Truman dutifully reported to a meeting in Pendergast's office. There he told Pendergast's friends they could get contracts if they were low bidders, but they would not get paid unless they met the specifications of his bipartisan board of engineers. Pendergast turned to the contractors. "I told you he's the contrariest man in the state of Missouri," he said. Afterward Pendergast told Truman, "You carry out the agreement you made with the people of Jackson County," and, according to Truman, "I never heard anything from him again."

In 1930 he was re-elected presiding judge by a huge majority. By that time Jackson County had one of the best road systems in the country and several new public buildings. He had organized the Greater Kansas City Regional Planning Association, partly to help fight the Depression which had suddenly hit the country. He was as tireless as he was honest. He traveled over every inch of the 350 miles of county roads with his two engineers, and insisted on getting every farmer in Jackson County within two and a half miles of a concrete road. Before building the new courthouse he made a 24,000-mile auto trip through the Southwest, Midwest, and East looking at other courthouses, talking to architects and incidentally getting acquainted with the country. One sight he saw everywhere: lines of unemployed men waiting for relief payments.

America, 1935. Unemployed men in New York.

And in one of the hundreds of "Hoovervilles."

Europe, 1935. German troops goose-step before Adolf Hitler.

On the basis of the job he had done as presiding judge, Harry Truman was entitled to a reasonable expectation of moving up the political ladder. He loyally supported Pendergast even when he did not agree with his choice of candidates. In 1932 he was a member of the Missouri delegation to the Democratic National Convention. Tom Pendergast tried to win support for an absurd old warhorse named Jim Reed, a former senator with a golden voice and an abhorrence of progress. Not only did Reed get few votes in the convention that nominated Franklin D. Roosevelt, but back home in Missouri he backed Pendergast's enemy Bennett Champ Clark for the Senate against his own former law partner, Charles M. Howell. Truman campaigned for Howell, who, however, lost to Clark.

The next spring the country began to breathe the exhilarating political air of the New Deal. The Depression was at its worst, but a strong wave of hope was sweeping out from Washington. Truman accepted an appointment without pay as Federal Re-Employment Director for Missouri. Harry Hopkins, Roosevelt's right-hand man, came out to confer with him, and found him already a confirmed New Dealer. In fact, as Truman himself said, he had put a New Deal-type program into effect in Jackson County with his public works projects. Speaking at Columbia in January of 1934, he subscribed to the proposal that work be spread by cutting down working hours, and went so far as to say: "Let's cut the work day to two hours and give the same wage we used to earn for a ten-hour day . . . We are now going about the job of redistributing wealth that was amassed in the robust years, but thank heaven we are going about it more peacefully than was done in Russia, Italy and Germany." The cloudy economics were part of the naïve liberal ideology of 1934.

Other winds of change were blowing in Jackson County. Tom Pendergast had found it expedient to accept relations with Kansas City mobster chief Johnny Lazia. Old-fashioned graft in building contracts was supplemented with less savory corruption—prostitution and gambling, at first closely connected with illegal liquor, but outliving repeal. This aspect of Pendergast rule was attracting attention beyond that accorded to the older, more accepted forms. The heat, in fact, was on, though it would take some time for it to reach explosive proportions. A federal grand jury indicted Lazia for income-tax evasion, but the gangster got out on appeal in time to help Pendergast smash reform opposition in the March municipal elections in Kansas City. Four people were killed as Lazia's hoodlums openly shot and

FROM MISSOURI TO WASHINGTON

slugged opposition campaign workers. It was worse than a crime, it was a blunder, and it roused a storm of indignation.

As Pendergast's reputation darkened, he began to experience trouble recruiting candidates. This was ironic, because 1934 was a great Democratic year, with the New Deal—which Pendergast disliked intensely–at the pinnacle of its appeal. A U. S. Senate seat, held by an obsolete Republican named Roscoe C. Patterson, was an obvious Democratic prize. Pendergast thought, with ponderous lack of imagination, of old Jim Reed, but Reed turned it down. So did Joe Shannon, the old Rabbit chief, now a congressman. So did James P. Aylward, Democratic State Chairman. Pendergast was in a quandary.

The grand jury that had hung an indictment on Johnny Lazia had taken a look into the Jackson County administration. It had promptly received a letter from Judge Truman offering to appear and waive immunity, "inviting the closest investigation because I am proud of the county court." He was not summoned, and the grand jury found no word of censure for the county administration.

Pendergast took a long look at his bespectacled, Anglo-Saxon, Baptist, Masonic, and Reserve Officer presiding judge. The name of Truman was totally unknown outside Jackson County, but at least it was a name without a blemish. In the vacuum Pendergast had come up with on the senatorial nomination, Truman was a *faute-de-mieux* best.

Aylward and Jim Pendergast waylaid Truman in a hotel in Sedalia, where he had gone on a speaking engagement. To their surprise, they had to do some persuading. Truman had been hoping only a few weeks earlier to get Pendergast's backing for a newly created congressional seat, and had been disappointed to find the boss already committed to someone else. He protested honestly to Aylward and Jim Pendergast that he could not afford an expensive statewide campaign. But the attraction of a U. S. Senate seat was too dazzling to turn down, and he agreed to give it a try.

His chances of winning the nomination did not look bright. Two veteran congressmen, John J. Cochran of St. Louis, and Jacob L. Milligan of Richmond, Missouri, were in the field. Senator Bennett Champ Clark, of a famous Democratic family politically based in St. Louis, supported Milligan. Pendergast was swiftly hung around Truman's neck, with special emphasis on the violent Kansas City election. Truman's somewhat disingenuous response was that he lived and voted in Independence, not Kansas City. He also pointed out that his opponents had in the past sought Pendergast support, as indeed anybody wanting to run for office as a Democrat in Missouri was likely to do. On the positive side, he was as wholehearted a New Dealer as his two opponents, Tom Pendergast notwithstanding, and he knew all the "court-house gangs" in the rural counties. Finally, he was a vigorous and effective campaigner, with his own style. Traveling the state by auto, he made as many as sixteen speeches a day, in cities, towns, hamlets and "wide places in the road." The rural counties proved the key to the election, as the rival Kansas City and St. Louis machines delivered almost equally massive and one-sided votes to their own choice—"voting the graveyards," according to well-founded rumor. Truman got over 130,000 votes in Jackson County, and fewer than 4000 in St. Louis. The *St. Louis Post-Dispatch* termed the result a demonstration of the power of machine politics, calling Truman "an obscure man . . . scarcely known outside the confines of Jackson County." But the *Kansas City Star,* despite its strenuous opposition to Pendergast, admitted that Judge Truman was a "capable and honest public official . . . a man of unimpeachable character and integrity."

The election was an anticlimax, Truman beating Senator Patterson by a quarter of a million.

That winter a jubilant Truman family—Harry, Bess, Bess's mother, and ten-year-old Margaret—arrived in Washington and after suitable expressions of pained surprise at Washington rents, settled in a modest apartment in Tilden Gardens.

The 1934 elections had been a Democratic sweep and Harry Truman was one of no fewer than thirteen freshman senators, all Democrats, who were sworn in on January 3, 1935. Though he was fifty years old and had experienced ordeal by fire in the Argonne Forest and Missouri politics, he was "as timid as a country boy." Before leaving home he had taken pains to study up on every one of his colleagues.

Several older senators went out of their way to give him help, especially Burton K. Wheeler of Montana, J. Ham Lewis of Illinois, and Carl Hayden of Arizona. Ham Lewis told him, "For the first six months you'll wonder how you got here, and after that you'll wonder how the rest of us got here."

Some of his colleagues, he observed, were unassuming, conscientious and hard-working, and accounted for most of the business done by the Senate. Others, among whom the most notorious was the improbable Huey Long of Louisiana, got most of the publicity. There was little doubt about which

Senator and Mrs. Truman. His election was almost a foregone conclusion after an electrifying victory in the Democratic primary. One of thirteen freshman senators, he felt "as timid as a country boy arriving on the campus of a great university." But he soon made himself at home in the Senate, winning a reputation as a four-square New Deal liberal.

Margaret Truman, the President's only child, was ten years old when her family moved from their home in Independence to a furnished apartment in Tilden Gardens, Washington, D.C. Accustomed to the free, easygoing life of a large house in Missouri, Margaret recalled that she hated the cooped-up, lonely feeling of their second-floor Washington apartment.

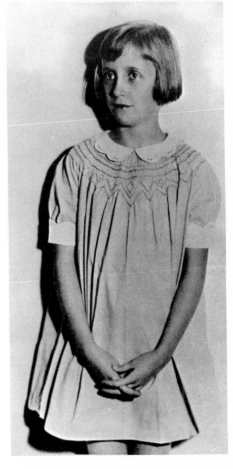

model of U. S. Senator Harry Truman would adopt. Roosevelt's State of the Union message, calling for basic reforms to replace the temporary emergency measures of the early New Deal, was followed the same afternoon by the introduction of a long list of bills and resolutions in the Senate. That night conscientious Senator Truman carried an armload of papers home to Tilden Gardens, a practice he did not realize would continue for eighteen years.

He began to feel that "I was now where I really belonged." His colleagues came to share the conviction. One day, in the course of a discussion on the floor he supplied a certain piece of needed information, and was gratified to have Senator Arthur H. Vandenberg of Michigan, one of the leading Republican members, comment: "When the Senator from Missouri makes a statement like that, we can take it for the truth."

He voted down the line for the New Deal—Wagner Labor Relations Act, Social Security, flood control, housing, replacements for the Agricultural Adjustment Act, the Wage-and-Hour Law, and many more. He voted against President Roosevelt's express wishes on only one bill, a very interesting one. Veterans' organizations had campaigned long and intensively for early payment of a bonus, amounting to several hundred dollars per man, which had been promised by the government to World War I soldiers, but which was not due until 1945. The cost was over $2,000,000,000, an amount which the congressional sponsors of the bill proposed to raise by barefaced inflation of the currency. Roosevelt, persuaded by old-fashioned orthodox economists who were horrified by the specter of a budget deficit, not only vetoed the bill but made his veto emphatic by addressing a joint session of Congress in person. But Harry Truman and many other senators and congressmen, most of whom also believed in balanced budgets, could not resist the political pressure and the human appeal of veterans who badly needed the money and who were sure to pump it into an economy hungering for it. For the first time in his administration, Roosevelt had the entire press backing him. Even the small liberal periodicals were sure he was right. But Roosevelt, the press and the little liberal magazines were wrong. The soldier's bonus, which the House passed over the veto, but which the Senate then killed, was one of the best anti-depression measures taken during the New Deal. Senator Truman voted with the Senate minority to override, and the next year, when the bill was introduced again, helped get it passed over the veto.

He was fortunate in committee appointments, landing on the important

Appropriations Committee and the Interstate Commerce Committee. He never missed a meeting of the Appropriations Committee, and through his zealous attendance became an expert on federal fiscal administration. On the Interstate Commerce Committee he vigorously backed the Wheeler-Rayburn bill to break up utilities holding companies. A huge lobbying effort led by such Wall Streeters as Wendell Willkie, John Foster Dulles, and John W. Davis blanketed the nation with propaganda, warning people that their utilities stocks would become worthless. Truman received over 30,000 letters and telegrams from constituents. He burned them, and continued to press the fight till the bill was passed. Together with Republican Senator Warren R. Austin of Vermont he wrote a bill making the Civil Aeronautics Agency a quasi-judicial body. Conservative Senator Pat McCarran, seeking to water down the measure, maneuvered to keep Truman off the joint Senate-House conference group working on it. But Truman's Missouri colleague, Bennett Champ Clark, who had campaigned against him in 1934, helped him get named to the group and block the McCarran attempt. He worked hard on the Transportation Act of 1940, ransacking the Library of Congress for information, and becoming vice-chairman of the subcommittee in charge.

In his first term Senator Truman cast a significant vote on foreign policy —to end the embargo Congress had placed on arms shipments abroad, which contributed to the defeat of the democratic side in the Spanish Civil War.

But after six years of unremitting hard work and effective contributions to reform legislation, Harry Truman found himself in such deep political trouble at home in Missouri that most of his friends urged him not to seek renomination.

The trouble was Pendergast. A new grand-jury investigation of fraud in the 1936 state elections had uncovered glaring corroboration of old charges of "ghost votes." Worse followed when the federal district attorney disclosed a sensational piece of graft on the part of Tom Pendergast, whose mania for betting on the horses had run him deep into debt. In January 1935, the month that Truman took his seat in the Senate, Pendergast made a deal in a Chicago hotel room. The bribe he accepted came not from the underworld but from several of the nation's leading insurance firms. Every week a man took the train from Chicago to Kansas City with a bundle of cash. Ultimately Pendergast collected, and gambled away, $430,000 of $750,000 promised him. In 1939, sick and beaten, old Tom pleaded guilty and went to jail for fifteen months.

That was bad enough, but Truman made it worse. At the height of the
investigation the term of Federal District Attorney Maurice Milligan, who
was prosecuting the case, ran out. Roosevelt sent Milligan's name to the
Senate for reappointment. Because Milligan was from western Missouri,
Truman considered that he should have been consulted, as in ordinary circumstances he would have been. He went so far as to speak and vote against
the reappointment. His was the sole vote cast against it, which looked like
barefaced service to a boss. It was rather the first major display of a Truman
political shortcoming—a trigger temper that made him react impulsively
when reflection would have been the better part of valor. It may also have
been an example of another fault—a blind loyalty to friends.

In 1940 Maurice Milligan announced his candidacy for Truman's Senate
seat. So did Governor Lloyd C. Stark. Stark was a popular American Legion-
naire with strong financial backing, a good record as governor, and a promise
of support from Roosevelt who, figuring that Truman was politically dead,
used a not-very-subtle method of pressuring him to withdraw. He quietly sent
word that Truman could have a seat on the Interstate Commerce Commission.

That did it. If there was anything Truman resented, it was a suggestion
that he should back away from a fight because he was likely to lose. He
sent word to the White House that he was going to run for re-election if he
only got one vote. Roosevelt decided to keep hands off the Missouri primary.

How far Truman was aware of Pendergast's various malfeasances is un-
certain. Old Tom's bribe-taking was a new development and Truman may
at first have found the accusation hard to believe. Pendergast had never asked
him to do anything dishonest. (Later, in the 1948 campaign, columnist-
historian Gerald Johnson defended Truman on Pendergast corruption by
declaring, "Harry was just playing the piano in the joint. He didn't know
what was going on upstairs.")

Truman plunged into the uphill fight with his usual vigor. He had a
few things going for him. Though the Pendergast machine lay in ruins, he
still had friends. Headed by Harry Vaughan, an old buddy of the 129th, they
opened a headquarters in a rented building at Sedalia and began canvassing
for contributions and campaign workers. As a consistently liberal Senator,
Truman had a record to point to. New Deal help for farmers was popular
in the rural counties of Missouri. His stand on the veterans' bonus helped.
Organized labor was ready to support a man who had voted for the Wagner

Boss Tom Pendergast went on trial for income-tax evasion in 1939, the charge growing out of an enormous bribe he had accepted to help pay off gambling debts. Above, he confers with his son, Tom Pendergast, Jr., center, and his nephew Jim Pendergast, left. It was Jim Pendergast, a fellow officer in the 129th F.A., who got Truman started in politics, and in 1940 the Pendergast label almost cost Truman his Senate seat.

World War II begins. Hitler's troops invaded Poland September 1, 1939. Poles fought heroically but were quickly overwhelmed.

Act and other labor and social-welfare legislation. When railroad management sought to get a national wage award canceled Truman had joined Burton K. Wheeler in strong and successful opposition, and the railroad brotherhoods had not forgotten. They put time and money into a broadside aimed at getting out the labor vote.

Finally, he had his own peculiar campaigning talent, now polished by experience. He knew how to reach a crowd with plain talk better than more naturally gifted speakers did with oratory. His technique was to keep the speech short, save enough time for hand-shaking, and then move out promptly. "Even if you have time left, leave," he advised another candidate. "If you have no place to go, you can always pull off the road and take a nap." He could not afford big expensive meetings, but his style was suited best to small crowds.

Several liberal Western senatorial colleagues came to Missouri to speak for him. Bennett Champ Clark made an eleventh-hour announcement in his favor. By the time primary day approached, underdog Truman was breathing on Governor Stark's neck, while Milligan had dropped to a poor third. Then Truman and his managers pulled off a major deal. In return for Truman's indorsement of the candidate for governor backed by Robert Hannegan, the St. Louis boss, Hannegan pledged his own backing to Truman. This key maneuver, made feasible by Truman's strong campaign, decided the primary. Truman carried St. Louis, previously conceded to Stark, by eight thousand votes—and won statewide by almost precisely that margin.

The nomination assured re-election, though he found his margin reduced from the quarter million of six years earlier to 44,000. This figure partly reflected the increased Republican strength nationwide in 1940, when Wendell Willkie, the ex-utilities magnate, made a surprisingly strong run against Roosevelt.

During the election campaign, Truman's Republican opponent, Manvelle Davis, made a speech quoting newspaper articles ("lies," says Truman bluntly in his *Memoirs*) from the *St. Louis Post-Dispatch* and the *Kansas City Star* on Truman's Pendergast-connected past. Present on the platform with Davis was Forrest C. Donnell, the Republican candidate for governor, and a Mason. Jim Wade, a Catholic friend of Truman, listened to Davis's aspersions, then buttonholed Donnell. Was it not true, he asked, that Senator Truman had been elected grand master of Masons? Donnell said it was. "Is it possible that he could have been elected to that office and be the low sort of person Manvelle Davis has been saying he is?"

Donnell replied, without hesitation, "Of course not."

Jim Wade broadcast Donnell's statement and, according to Truman, who derived great satisfaction from the incident, "it cost Davis thousands of votes."

Senator Truman returned to Washington vindicated by victory. Politicians had to feel respect for a man who had proved himself not only a fighter but a winner.

Yet the shadow of Tom Pendergast hung over him. He was "that Senator from Missouri, the one who was mixed up with the dirty politics and the crooked bosses." Faithful New Dealer though he was, he was held at arm's length by the New Dealers.

In the language of a later day, he needed a new image. It did not occur to Harry Truman to seek one, but early in his new term he began to acquire one, simply by doing what came naturally. Where he got it had to do with the very new and alarming situation the country found itself in as Congress opened in January 1941. Few Americans ever dreamed that the Maginot Line was part of the defense system of the U.S., but with the fall of France, Britain alone stood between a powerful, aggressive, thoroughly sinister Nazi Germany, and an America with an inadequate Navy and virtually non-existent Army and Air Force.

An almost panicky rush to build the nation's defenses included the first peacetime conscription act in history (September 1940) and huge appropriations, rushed through Congress with little opposition. In a fireside chat on December 29, 1940, Roosevelt called for an immense production effort not only to re-arm America swiftly but to provide an "arsenal of democracy" to sustain Britain and others fighting Hitler. In his annual message to the opening of Congress he recommended an imaginative program of "Lend Lease" to the Allies.

Some $16,500,000,000 already appropriated, plus a new $4,000,000,000 now requested for the Army and $7,000,000,000 for Lend-Lease, added up to $27,500,000,000, figures which made the New Deal agencies of the previous ten years look like tight-fisted misers. Yet where the press, the Republican opposition and not a few Democrats had expressed extreme apprehensions over the profligacy of the WPA, patriotic alarm now drowned out the few voices raised to question how this vast sum was to be spent.

Pearl Harbor. Japanese dive bombers and torpedo bombers carried out a devastating surprise attack on December 7, 1941, sinking or disabling nineteen warships, destroying 150 planes, killing 2335 U.S. soldiers and sailors, and precipitating America into global war.

The Truman Committee, which saved billions of dollars and many lives during World War II, was authorized following Senator Truman's personal fact-finding trip to defense plants, Army camps and installations. From left: Senators Joseph H. Ball, Mon C. Wallgren, Tom Connally, James M. Mead, Owen Brewster, and Chairman Truman, seated.

D-Day on Omaha Beach: GIs storm ashore from landing barges in the invasion of Europe.

A senator who had had personal experience with construction contracts might feel special concern. Senator Truman was aware, as many of his colleagues were not, that safeguards could be applied without delaying the program. He suspected that awarding practically all contracts to the biggest firms in order to "save time" was a mistake. The shortage of machine tools led the giant companies that were getting the contracts to buy up, and even requisition, machinery belonging to smaller companies and move it long distances, creating unemployment at the old site and a housing shortage at the new one.

Truman resolved to take a firsthand look at the whole pell-mell defense build-up. Driving out of Washington all by himself, he headed down through Maryland to Florida, then westward to Texas, up through Oklahoma to Nebraska and back through Wisconsin, Michigan, and New York. He visited Army camps and installations, and plants working on the new defense contracts, and so far as possible kept his identity secret.

He returned "convinced that something needed to be done fast," to halt what threatened to be a runaway of waste, inefficiency and probably corruption. These very labels had been extravagantly pinned on Truman as a New Dealer and a Pendergast man. A quite different, much more accurate, picture of him was about to emerge.

On February 10, 1941, he submitted a draft resolution calling for a special Senate committee to investigate the national-defense effort. In his speech he cited impressive authenticating facts, including much of his own observation, and pointed out the dangers inherent in awarding the majority of contracts to a small number of very large firms. The resolution, calling for a committee of five senators with an appropriation of $25,000, went to the Senate Committee on Audit and Control of Contingent Expense, of which Senator James F. Byrnes of South Carolina was chairman. Byrnes, whose path was to cross Truman's in the years ahead, apparently did not take the proposed investigation very seriously, because he first whittled the appropriation to $10,000, and only after some argument agreed to a compromise figure of $15,000. At the same time he expanded the committee to seven.

Truman, who as author of the resolution automatically became chairman of the committee, took pains with its makeup. He consulted not only Vice-President Henry A. Wallace, presiding officer of the Senate, but Majority Leader Alben Barkley and Minority Leader Charles L. McNary, and even President Roosevelt. The committee as finally picked included several of the ablest men in the Senate: Tom Connally, Carl Hatch, James Mead, Mon Wallgren, Joseph Ball, and Owen Brewster. Truman next called on Attorney General Robert H. Jackson to find a top-flight attorney as chief investigator, and got Hugh Fulton, one of Jackson's own assistants, paying $9000 of the $15,000 appropriation for his salary.

Within a few weeks the Truman Committee was making headlines, not with sensational or exaggerated charges, but with findings which stood up to newspaper and congressional scrutiny and led to important revisions in defense-spending methods. The breakneck pace at which the Army was building camps to house its new recruits had created a shortage of construction machinery. To meet the shortage the Army was renting machinery by bid, which sent the cost way up. A check showed that contractors were earning three and four times as much on three-month "cost-plus" jobs for the government as they had formerly made in a year of ordinary work. Some of the building-trades unions were charging outrageous fees for work permits, and so slowing down recruitment of needed skilled and even unskilled labor.

Early in the committee's work an unforeseen problem fell within its jurisdiction. The United Mine Workers, one of the strongest unions in the country, struck to back up a demand for a wage increase. The interruption of coal-mining was of utmost seriousness to the whole defense effort, and Senator Truman boldly moved in on the problem. Summoning John L. Lewis, the president of the United Mine Workers, and representatives of the two large management groups, he learned that the northern mine operators were willing to meet the union's demands but the southern were holding out. Truman notified the mine operators that unless coal was being mined within twenty-four hours the owners would be summoned before the committee "to show why their wage dispute should come ahead of the national safety." The deadlock was broken, and the strike ended that night.

The Truman Committee's original shoestring appropriation was rapidly augmented, permitting the hiring of a top-notch team of investigators. Truman himself worked with his usual energy and conscientiousness, and the publicity resulting from the committee's success soon brought in volunteer complaints and reports, especially from small businessmen who had been shut out on contract awards. Moving out of Washington the committee held hearings around the country. It made regular reports to the Senate. It forced the rewriting of major contracts, the expansion of aluminum production, and finally in a particularly significant investigation, caused the reorganization of a major executive wartime agency, the Office of Production Management, into a more efficient War Production Board.

By the time the Japanese attacked Pearl Harbor, the Truman Committee had become one of the most important investigating committees in the history of Congress. With the nation now actually at war, the potential for waste was multiplied. It was no longer merely a question of giving away excessive profits. The committee reached into the field of allocations. In the early months of 1942 it discovered that quantities of war-essential steel, copper, tin, and lead were going to business-as-usual toy firms turning out electric trains and little red wagons. Next it turned up the fact that though many business executives were patriotically serving the government for the nominal fee of $1 a year, some were serving their own companies and industries better than the government. It revealed to an appalled public, over bitter Navy protests, the secret that German U-boats had sunk more shipping tonnage in 1942 than the country had produced. The spotlight thus turned on the U-boat menace led to development of overdue countermeasures, saving many lives and contributing significantly to final victory.

Truman had no hesitation about getting tough with generals, admirals, and industrial tycoons. When Curtiss-Wright and the Army both found nothing wrong with an airplane plant that was producing defective engines, the Truman Committee published its own investigation, condemning four hundred of the engines. The committee's investigators reported that the Martin B-26 bomber had too short a wingspread. Glenn Martin, president of the company, testified that the blueprints for the plane were too far along to change. Truman told Martin that the committee would see to it that unless the wingspread was lengthened the planes would not be purchased. Martin agreed to make the change.

Only once did Truman accept an evasion. His investigators had appeared at the gates of a giant new plant outside the tiny town of Oak Ridge, Tennessee, and demanded entrance to find out what was being produced inside. They were refused on orders of the Secretary of War. Truman took the question up at once in Washington, and was told by Secretary Stimson that the Oak Ridge plant involved "the greatest project in the history of the world," and that it was "most top secret." Stimson did not absolutely refuse to tell Truman what the project was, but expressed the hope that the committee would not press its investigation. Truman accepted Stimson's declaration and called off his investigators.

By the beginning of the election year of 1944 Harry Truman was one of the leading figures in the Senate, his Pendergast past eclipsed by the Truman Committee's accomplishments. But it was considerably to his surprise that he began to hear his name mentioned as a candidate for Vice-President. Modesty aside, he was thoroughly happy in the Senate. Even hints from Robert Hannegan, the St. Louis boss who had become national chairman of the party, failed to impress him. Besides, several other names were being mentioned ahead of his.

The problem of the vice-presidency arose because Henry Wallace, the incumbent, was considered too flamboyant a liberal for a wartime ticket. Roosevelt's own nomination, precedent-shattering though it was, was inevitable. What the big-city bosses and other party leaders wanted for the No. 2 position was a moderate, middle-of-the-road liberal, preferably from the Midwest or West, who had not already offended southern conservatives.

There was no lack of volunteers. After brushing aside all suggestions from friends, Truman was at home in Independence packing to leave for the Chicago convention when the telephone rang. It was James F. Byrnes, an old senatorial colleague, ncw head of the Office of War Mobilization. Byrnes, who had been prominently mentioned as a vice-presidential possibility, informed Truman that he had Roosevelt's backing, and wanted Truman to make his nominating speech. Truman was glad to oblige. Before he could finish packing he had another call. Senate Majority Leader Alben Barkley, another good friend, wanted Truman to make a nominating speech for him!

But when Truman arrived in Chicago he found himself the object of attentions from a succession of labor leaders. Sidney Hillman, head of the CIO's Political Action Committee, invited him to breakfast. Truman asked Hillman if he would support Byrnes. Hillman said he would not, and asserted that if Wallace could not be nominated, there were only two men he would support—Justice William O. Douglas of the Supreme Court and Senator Harry S Truman. Later Philip Murray, president of the CIO, and A. F. Whitney, head of the Railroad Trainmen, sought him out and repeated exactly what Hillman had said—that if Wallace did not make it, they would support either Douglas or Truman and nobody else.

Next morning William Green, head of the AFL, invited Truman to breakfast at the Palmer House. Green's message was slightly different: he said the AFL would support Truman, period. As they talked, Senator Millard F. Tydings of Maryland strolled over and asked Truman to come and meet

The Vice-presidential Sweepstakes: Byrnes, Douglas, LEFT, Barkley, Wallace, RIGHT, were all favored ahead of Truman, who stubbornly refused to be a candidate until he heard Roosevelt on the phone to Democratic Chairman Bob Hannegan: "Tell him if he wants to break up the Democratic party in the middle of a war, that's his responsibility."

his state delegation at a neighboring table. Truman accompanied Tydings to his table, where to Truman's astonishment Tydings introduced him as "the Maryland candidate for Vice-President."

To every one of his callers Truman repeated that he was not a candidate, and faithfully reported each conversation to Byrnes. Byrnes' reaction was that it would all be straightened out as soon as Roosevelt made his preference known.

The next few days were bewildering. Hannegan called on Truman and gave him the incredible news that Roosevelt "wanted" him. This was hard to believe for several reasons, including the fact that he was by no means on intimate terms with the White House. Roosevelt had refused to back him for re-election to the Senate in 1940, and the Truman Committee had more than once rapped the knuckles of the Executive branch. Further, Truman was aware of a letter Roosevelt had written stating that he would be satisfied with either Wallace or Douglas. When Hannegan showed him a penciled note saying, "Bob, it's Truman. F.D.R.," he remained skeptical.

In this mood he declared out of order a motion by the Missouri delegation of which he was chairman, to indorse their favorite son for Vice-President. The Missourians, for once in their lives united, inveigled their chairman out of the room long enough to pass the resolution.

Behind the baffling development of the Truman boom lay a tangle of conflicting calculations and sentiments on the part of the leading Democratic bosses and Roosevelt. FDR favored Wallace, but half-persuaded that Wallace would fatally weaken the ticket, had given tentative approval to several others, including Byrnes, Truman, and Douglas. New York boss Ed Flynn raised a serious objection to Byrnes—he was not only a southerner, but also a fallen-away Catholic and therefore would endanger not only Negro but Catholic support in the big cities. And labor, at least the CIO, refused to have him.

That left Truman and Douglas, with FDR apparently leaning toward the Supreme Court justice. In a note to Hannegan before the convention he mentioned both, with Douglas's name first.

Douglas's attitude, however, was not known, and in any case he was not at the convention. When Hannegan arrived in Chicago and assessed the battle shaping up between Byrnes and Wallace, he felt he had to play a trump card quick. Roosevelt's train, en route to the West Coast, would pass through Chicago. Hannegan arranged a secret meeting with FDR at a siding, and got the President to write a new note putting Truman's name ahead of Douglas's. This note, less ambiguous than the "Bob, it's Truman" scrawl, was a powerful weapon. Hannegan held it until Wednesday, two days before the nomination, then released it to the press. Its immediate effect was to torpedo Byrnes, its secondary effect to put a heavy damper on Henry Wallace's hopes. It did not, however, extinguish them. Wallace still had many delegates lined up, enjoyed enthusiastic labor support, and regardless of all the notes, was known to be acceptable to FDR. And to Hannegan's intense frustration, Truman, puzzled but stubborn, still held out.

On Thursday afternoon, Hannegan made a desperation move. Inviting Truman to his suite at the Blackstone, he put through a long distance call to Roosevelt, now in San Diego. Truman sat on one twin bed and Hannegan on the other. Everybody else in the room held his breath as Roosevelt's familiar boom came over the wire: "Bob, have you got that fellow lined up yet?"

"No," Hannegan replied, and unconsciously echoing Tom Pendergast twenty years earlier added, "He's the contrariest Missouri mule I've ever dealt with."

"Well," said Roosevelt, "you tell him that if he wants to break up the Democratic party in the middle of a war, that's his responsibility."

Truman sat still, then stood up and began pacing the room. No one said a word.

"Well," he brought out at last, "if that is the situation, I'll have to say yes, but why the hell didn't he tell me in the first place?"

Truman's first business as a candidate was to go to the Stevens Hotel and break the news to Byrnes. Embittered by what he felt was a stab in the back from Roosevelt, Byrnes withdrew his name from the convention. Truman's next business was to find someone to make a nomination speech, not too easy at this late date. His old Missouri foe, now friend, Bennett Champ Clark, took the assignment.

By the time the balloting began, Hannegan had passed the word on Roosevelt's choice. Wallace led on the first ballot, 420½ to Truman's 319½, and the gallery was in an uproar. But on the second ballot, minor candidates and favorite sons began swinging over, and Truman was nominated.

The long tension exploded in a pandemonium that was exceptional even for an American political convention. Truman delivered an extremely brief acceptance speech and the noise redoubled. Reporters, cameramen, radio

The Nominee. As Mayor Kelly of Chicago raised Truman's hand in token of victory, few of the delegates to the convention realized that they had nominated not only a Vice-President, but a President.

Campaign of '44: Truman did nearly all the work, freeing FDR for war leadership. Signing autographs for a group of youngsters in Madison, Wis.

January 20, 1945: The inauguration was held on the south portico of the White House instead of at the Capitol, in deference to Roosevelt's physical handicap and general health. Truman noted that it was the third wartime inaugural.

broadcasters and guards converged on the Truman family. The building re-
verberated with flash bulbs. Police and Secret Service men fought to form
a cordon. Bess managed to get her husband's ear over the din: "Are we
going to have to go through this all the rest of our lives?" she wanted to know.

It was not till mid-August, when Roosevelt returned from military conferences in Hawaii, that the presidential and vice-presidential nominees
got together to plan strategy. Their meeting was over luncheon on the White
House grounds, under the magnolia tree that Andrew Jackson planted in
memory of his wife Rachel. It was agreed that Truman would do all the
campaigning, leaving Roosevelt free to devote his energies to the war. Truman's main theme in his speeches was ironic in view of the sequel. He ham-
mered at the idea that no man could acquire overnight the long grasp of
wartime problems, the familiarity with Allied leaders and their thinking, that
FDR possessed. His target was Governor Thomas E. Dewey of New York,
the Republican candidate for President. Few noticed that most of what he
said applied to himself.

Despite a vigorous campaign by Dewey, the Roosevelt-Truman ticket won
without difficulty. On a snowy January 20, 1945, Harry Truman stood on
the south portico of the White House beside Franklin D. Roosevelt for the
third wartime inauguration, the first two being Madison's in 1813 and Lincoln's in 1865. As soon as possible after the official White House luncheon
Truman slipped away to telephone his mother at Grandview. "Now you
behave yourself," Martha warned him.

Almost immediately after the inauguration Roosevelt left for the Yalta
meeting with Stalin and Churchill, on which he reported to Congress in a
joint session on March 1. On March 30 he left for his Warm Springs, Georgia,
home to rest.

Two weeks later, on April 12, Vice-President Truman finished a letter he
was writing to his mother and sister as he presided over the Senate during
a "windy senator's" speech. Toward five o'clock he adjourned the Senate
and headed for the office of his good friend, Speaker of the House Sam
Rayburn, for the usual swapping of information, flavored with a peg of
bourbon. But this afternoon Sam told Truman as soon as he came in the
door that Steve Early, the President's press secretary, had telephoned and
asked that Truman call him back at once.

"Please come right over," Early's strained voice was saying a few moments
later, "and come in through the main Pennsylvania Avenue entrance."

Vice-presidential Concerto. Truman, an accomplished pianist, played an impromptu duet with comedian Jack Benny at the National Press Club a week after the inauguration.

Roosevelt at Yalta. The strain of twelve years in the White House showed unmistakably as the sixty-three-year-old President posed with Churchill and Stalin. Two months later he was dead—without ever having told Truman about the atomic-bomb project.

Truman figured that Roosevelt must have returned suddenly from Warm Springs for the funeral of a friend who had just died in Washington, and that he wanted to discuss something before going back to finish his vacation. He was puzzled by Early's request that he use the main entrance to the White House, because previously he had always used the side, or unofficial entrance. Going directly from Rayburn's office through the basement of the Capitol Building to his car, he arrived at the White House alone, without his usual Secret Service man.

He was escorted to Mrs. Roosevelt's study on the second floor. Mrs. Roosevelt, her son-in-law Colonel John Boettiger, her daughter Anna Roosevelt Boettiger, and Steve Early were there. Mrs. Roosevelt, calm and dignified, placed her hand on Truman's shoulder. "Harry," she said simply, "the President is dead."

Stunned, Truman at last said, "Is there anything I can do for you?"

To which Mrs. Roosevelt replied, "Is there anything *we* can do for *you?* For you are the one in trouble now."

April–May 1945

GREATNESS THRUST UPON HIM

With a suddenness that shocked the world, the brilliant chief Franklin D. Roosevelt was gone and in his place was a little man with glasses.

The very name Harry Truman was unknown outside America, and not too well known inside. No one had had time to get used to Truman as Vice-President. When newspaper correspondents, columnists, and other members of the political cognoscenti recovered from their initial stupefaction, they turned on the new President a unanimous gaze of condescending sympathy. Poor little fellow—how could he step into the giant shoes of Roosevelt? The Truman Committee, which had won him respect, supplied an inadequate glamour for the presidency.

The estimate of Truman as a colorless and insignificant fellow, unhappily pushed into the spotlight of history, so dominated the thinking of the press and other Roosevelt-hypnotized observers that it was years before the real capacity, and even the real personality, of Harry Truman began to be appreciated. Yet from the very beginning of his presidency he acted exactly like himself.

In the face of the staggering impact of Mrs. Roosevelt's announcement, he displayed a remarkable aplomb. Going to the President's office at the west end of the White House he gave all the necessary orders, summoning the Cabinet, Chief Justice Harlan F. Stone, the appropriate congressional leaders, and Bess and twenty-one-year-old Margaret. At the same time he ordered an Air Force plane to take Mrs. Roosevelt to Warm Springs.

At a tense and silent gathering in the Cabinet Room the Chief Justice administered the oath. Cabinet members and senators in turn pressed Truman's hand, often too overcome to say a word. Then all except the Cabinet left and Truman took his place at the head of the Cabinet table. Just as he did so Steve Early entered with an urgent question. The newspaper correspondents wanted to know if the San Francisco Conference, called to write the charter for the United Nations, would assemble as planned on April 25. Truman neither hesitated nor asked anybody's advice. He told Early to tell the press that the San Francisco Conference would go ahead as scheduled.

It was a significant incident, and underlined what he now told the glittering collection of Roosevelt appointees he faced. He told them that he would assume full responsibility for policy decisions. They could differ with him, and he welcomed the expression of their opinions, but once he had made a decision he expected their support.

The members of the Cabinet departed, probably with mixed feelings, and without a word to Truman except for Secretary of War Stimson, who told the new President that he wanted to speak to him soon about the development of a new explosive of "almost unbelievable destructive power." For the time being that was all Stimson said.

The next day, Truman's first full one as President, began with an early morning walk, breakfast, a drive to the White House and a whirlwind round of conferences. The first was with Secretary of State Stettinius, who gave him an up-to-date report on foreign affairs. Stettinius laid emphasis on the problem of Poland and the small East European states which the victorious Russian armies were overrunning and apparently staking out for Communism. Next he met with General George C. Marshall, Admiral Ernest J. King and other top officers for a military briefing. This proved surprisingly pessimistic. Despite the fact that American troops had reached the Elbe two days before, and that German resistance was crumbling rapidly, the official military estimate of the resistance potential of Nazi fanatics was six months. Turning to the Pacific, where enemy fanaticism was a good deal more real, and where an appalling battle was raging on the island of Okinawa, the generals calculated that final victory could not be achieved in less than eighteen months.

Truman drove to the Capitol to lunch with a group of leading Senators and Representatives and arrange to address a joint session two days later. He could have merely notified Congress of his intention, but as an old Senate hand he realized the value of enlisting co-operative approval. At 2:30 he was back in the White House to meet Jimmy Byrnes, whom he had caused to be summoned from his South Carolina home. He told Byrnes he was planning to make him Secretary of State after the San Francisco

White House, April 12, 1945: Amid a hushed gathering of Cabinet members and leading congressmen, Harry Truman took the oath of office as President from Chief Justice
Harlan F. Stone. Only two hours before, a tight-voiced Truman had telephoned Bess
and Margaret to summon them to the White House, impatiently brushing off Margaret's
casual chatter in order to quickly break the news to his wife. During the swearing-in
ceremony, Bess stood directly behind the President, with Margaret between him and
the Chief Justice.

Roosevelt's funeral, ABOVE, and burial in Hyde Park, BELOW, plunged the government and nation into mourning, and Harry Truman into a welter of terrific problems, with little time for briefing.

Trouble in Europe: Ambassador to Moscow Averell Harriman, right, with Soviet Foreign Commissar V. M. Molotov. Russian determination to communize the governments of Poland and other East European states was one of Truman's first and most difficult problems.

Trouble in Asia: Chinese Nationalist Foreign Minister T. V. Soong was among a crowd of foreign visitors who filled Truman's hectic first days. BELOW, Soong chats with the new President and Cabinet members Stimson, left, and Forrestal. Soong's mission was to get U.S. gold to rescue China's currency.

Conference, and that he wanted to see the notes Byrnes had taken at Yalta. An important reason for his decision on Byrnes was that in the absence of a Vice-President the next person in line for the presidential succession was the Secretary of State. Although Edward R. Stettinius might prove a competent Secretary, he had never held elective office, whereas Byrnes had been a senator as well as a Supreme Court Justice, and had stood close to Roosevelt for many years.

At 3:30 Stettinius returned with Charles Bohlen, the State Department's expert on Russia, and a typed memorandum on foreign relations. They discussed the Polish problem, which from the American point of view revolved around the makeup of the new Polish government. At Yalta Stalin had agreed to a democratic government for Poland, but his interpretation of the word "democratic" left much to be desired, and it was becoming clear that what he wanted was a pro-Russian government. The Polish government sitting in exile in London was anything but that, while the Russian-organized "Lublin government" was transparently Communist, and unrepresentative, and therefore unacceptable to the U.S.

Yet Truman felt the question was too critical for postponement. He already had a cable from Churchill recommending a joint British-American declaration and he now drafted a reply suggesting instead a fresh British-American message to Stalin. Truman proposed a joint committee of the pro-Russian Poles in power in Warsaw and the anti-Russian Poles in London. He also sent a message to Stalin. The U.S. wanted Russian Foreign Commissar Vyacheslav Molotov to attend the San Francisco Conference as a sign of serious Russian commitment and Stalin had agreed on condition that Molotov also have an opportunity to talk to the President. Truman accepted.

Throughout the day he busily devoured reports and memoranda in an effort to get abreast of all the enormous complications of wartime government. Despite fatigue, he took a bundle of papers home with him that night.

The pace hardly slackened the rest of the week. At the joint session of Congress he almost made a gaffe, and the voice of Speaker Sam Rayburn was heard over the nationwide radio hookup: "Just a minute, Harry, let me introduce you." He received congressional delegations and foreign ambassadors, signed his first bills, cast his first veto and held his first press conference as President. He made his first appointments—old friend John Snyder of St. Louis as Federal Loan Administrator, and old schoolmate

Charlie Ross as press secretary. He conferred on the budget with Budget Director Harold Smith and with Secretary of the Treasury Henry Morgenthau, talked with Rabbi Stephen Wise about refugees, with the commander of the American Legion about veterans' problems, and most important, with Averell Harriman, just returned from Moscow, about Russia and the Poles.

On Sunday, April 22, Molotov arrived. At the first meeting all went well with conversation restricted to generalities. But when an attempt was made to wrestle with the realities of the Polish question it became evident that Molotov and Stalin remained intransigent. Truman expressed his dissatisfaction so bluntly that Molotov exclaimed, "I have never been talked to like that in my life." To which Truman, President of the United States for eleven days, rejoined: "Carry out your agreements and you won't get talked to like that!"

Two days later a cable arrived from Stalin, arguing strongly, almost emotionally, Russia's need for a "friendly" government in Poland: "You demand too much of me . . . You demand that I renounce the interest of security of the Soviet Union, but I cannot turn against my country." It was a frank avowal, possibly intended to open the way for a diplomatic deal in terms of spheres of influence. But for Truman to abandon the Poles to Communism was out of the question. The Polish problem in fact was insoluble.

That evening Truman had a lengthy telephone conversation with Churchill about a German surrender offer which had come by way of Sweden from Hitler's lieutenant Heinrich Himmler. The transatlantic telephone cable did not yet exist, and the two statesmen had some difficulties with the radio transmission. Nevertheless, the dialogue went smoothly, reaching an agreement to give the Russians full notification and to insist that German surrender be made to all three major allies at once. This information, cabled to Stalin, brought a prompt expression of gratitude.

Next day Truman at last found time for Stimson and the atomic bomb.

The delay was not entirely owing to the pressure of more urgent business. It was due also to the fact that Truman's knowledge of the subject was so scanty that he was scarcely able to assess its importance in advance.

Henry L. Stimson was an old-fashioned public servant of ability and integrity. Seventy-seven years old, he had served in the Cabinets of Republican Presidents Taft and Hoover, and had been called out of retirement by Franklin D. Roosevelt sixteen months before Pearl Harbor. He had given a great deal of searching thought to the monster weapon which was being slowly forged in the laboratories in Chicago, Berkeley, and New York, in the giant industrial plants at Oak Ridge and Hanford, and in the assembly center at Los Alamos.

The memorandum he had prepared for the conference began:

"Within four months we shall in all probability have completed the most terrible weapon ever known in human history, one bomb of which could destroy a whole city."

As Truman listened intently, Stimson went on to make several major points:

Though development of the atomic bomb had been shared with Britain, the U.S. possessed a monopoly on its manufacture. This monopoly, however, was strictly temporary. Further, there was a danger that the process of manufacture, at present prohibitive, might become much cheaper, permitting many nations to make bombs. Given the gap between the world's technical and moral development, "modern civilization might be completely destroyed." Finally, Stimson foresaw enormous difficulties in the way of setting up a practical system of control through the United Nations.

Stimson's summation was a masterly one, yet its effect on Truman might have been different if one of the scientists had given it (General Leslie R. Groves, the military head of the Manhattan Project, was the only other person present.) Stimson, no scientist, regarded the bomb as simply a very large weapon, and this view carried over to Truman. The scientists had been carrying on an agitated discussion for some months. Many felt that with Nazi Germany defeated, and no atomic-bomb threat leveled at America, the U.S. should renounce use of its own bomb. Vice-President Henry Wallace had been well-informed and had had an important official connection with the project. Unaccountably, Roosevelt had neglected to have the new Vice-President even briefed, and although literally thousands of people—scientists, industrialists, engineers, government officials, military officers—knew about the bomb, Truman did not.

Groves had brought along a twenty-four-page summary of technical details which the new President was now given to read. Not surprisingly in the circumstances, subtleties that had potential political significance escaped Truman.

Whether he would have handled the bomb differently if he had had an opportunity for fuller acquaintance remains conjectural. But the tardiness

Fall of Berlin. Russian flag flew over the ruins of the Reichstag. Four-power Control Council that was set up at Yalta became a focus of Soviet-U.S. friction, ultimately leading to a major crisis for Truman.

Bloody Battle of Okinawa, which raged through Truman's first weeks as President, made it evident that an invasion of Japanese home islands would be costly. BELOW, infantrymen crawl up Jap escarpment behind a flame-throwing tank.

and haste of indoctrination may well have contributed to his unquestioning acceptance of the bomb's use as a combat weapon.

He had little time to reflect about anything. Events calling for major decisions were pressing hard. Churchill and his foreign secretary, Anthony Eden, were urging that U.S. forces try to liberate Prague ahead of the Russians—a potentially dangerous bit of chicanery that Eisenhower was resisting.

Churchill, who had failed in an earlier attempt to cajole Eisenhower into capturing Berlin ahead of the Russians, was growing alarmist in proportion to the success of Allied arms. The rapid Russian advance through East Germany led him to fear that "terrible things" had happened to the Germans. He pointed out that U.S. withdrawal to the line of demarcation fixed at the Quebec Conference the year before would mean "the tide of Russian domination sweeping forward 120 miles on a front of 300 or 400 miles." His forecast conceded Finland, Czechoslovakia, a "large part of Austria," and probably Trieste to the Russians, or at least to Communism. He had forebodings about Greece, Turkey, "and Constantinople." The last-ditch Nazi resistance that American military prognosis had overestimated was rapidly collapsing. Churchill feared that Russian, rather than British-U.S. power, would flow into the vacuum.

In response, Truman dispatched two diplomatic emissaries. To Moscow he sent Harry Hopkins, Roosevelt's top aide. To London went Joseph Davies, former Ambassador to Moscow. Stalin promised Hopkins he would install a "parliamentary" system in Poland like that of Czechoslovakia, Belgium, and Holland, but only offered four posts out of some twenty in the new Warsaw government to the London Poles. One real concession was won: Stalin agreed that in the United Nations the veto power should not be used to prevent discussion of a question.

Churchill grew emotional in his talk with Davies. He was very bitter about Marshal Tito of Yugoslavia, whom he correctly believed to be a Communist, but erroneously pictured as "completely under the domination of Moscow." He protested again U.S. adherence to the line of demarcation in Germany agreed to at Quebec, and Davies reported, "When I suggested that there had been express agreement as to these zones, he said that conditions had greatly changed."

A decision on Churchill's entreaty was made easier because military considerations, in the view of both Eisenhower and Marshall, were strongly opposed. It was soon apparent that things were not turning out quite as badly as Churchill anticipated, both Finland and ultimately Austria remaining independent and democratic.

As the emergency period of the new presidency passed, the members of Roosevelt's Cabinet resigned one by one. Among the leading new members were Byrnes at State, and Fred M. Vinson of Kentucky at Treasury. Vinson, an old friend of Truman's and an able public servant, succeeded Henry Morgenthau, who had recently put forward a plan to convert Germany into a pastoral land by shutting down the mines of the Ruhr and Saar. Roosevelt, Churchill, and Cordell Hull had all at one time taken the "Morgenthau Plan" seriously, but by the time Truman came into office its irrationality was recognized.

Truman had nearly completed his baptism of fire, but one experience remained—his first mistake. Following the Cabinet meeting on May 8, V-E Day, Foreign Economic Administrator Leo T. Crowley and Acting Secretary of State Joseph C. Grew called to ask him to sign an order which Roosevelt had approved but had postponed signing, authorizing a cutback on the volume of Lend-Lease sometime after Germany's surrender. Truman reached for a pen and signed. Crowley returned to his office and put an embargo on all shipments to Russia, Britain and other European nations, even causing some ships to be turned around and returned for unloading. The British protested, and the suspicious Russians jumped to the conclusion that the move was deliberate and aimed exclusively at them. Truman rescinded the order, and wrote himself a strong mental note not to sign anything without reading it.

Oddly enough, he had expressed a premonition about his "first mistake" in a letter that very morning, detailing for his mother and sister the complications of arranging V-E Day:

> Dear Mama & Mary:
>
>   I am sixty-one this morning, and slept in the President's room in the White House last night.
>
>   At 9:00 o'clock this morning I must make a broadcast to the country announcing the German surrender. The papers were signed yesterday morning and hostilities will cease on all fronts at midnight tonight. Isn't that some birthday present?
>
>   Have had one heck of a time with the Prime Minister of Great Britain. He, Stalin and the U. S. President made an agreement to release the

V-E Day. Truman, after lengthy negotiation with Churchill and Stalin over the timing of the announcement, proclaimed it at a special press conference, May 8, 1945, surrounded by Cabinet members and aides.

America celebrated—in New York's financial district and elsewhere—with a burst of patriotic pride and joy.

The United Nations is born. President Truman's first on-the-spot decision was that the UN planning conference should go forward on schedule despite Roosevelt's death. Two months later, he flew to San Francisco for the signing of the Charter. Secretary of State Stettinius signs as Truman looks on. BELOW, he chats with GIs home from the fighting front.

news all at once from the three capitals at an hour that would fit us all. We agreed on 9 a.m. Washington time which is 3 p.m. London and 4 p.m. Moscow time.

Mr. Churchill began calling me at daylight to know if we shouldn't make an immediate release without considering the Russians. He was refused and then he kept pushing me to talk to Stalin. He finally had to stick to the agreed plan—but he was mad as a wet hen.

Things have moved at a terrific rate here since April 12. Never a day has gone by that some momentous decision didn't have to be made. So far luck has been with me . . . I hope when the mistake comes it won't be too great to remedy.

We are looking forward to a grand visit with you . . .

Lots & lots of love to you both.

HARRY

The visit of Martha Young Truman and Mary Jane came four days later, at the end of the thirty-day mourning period for President Roosevelt. It involved a few complications of its own. Martha, ninety-two years old, was chagrined at seeing a crowd at the airport. "Fiddlesticks," she told her son, "why didn't you tell me there was going to be all this fuss, and I wouldn't have come."

She had already told her son, Vivian, to "tell Harry that if he puts me in the room with Lincoln's bed in it I'll sleep on the floor." This reaction was dictated not by awe but by political prejudice—Martha Truman was still bitter about the Civil War, and Vivian had been having a little fun with her. Actually the ladies were to share the Rose Room. After inspecting the bed in which not Lincoln, but several queens and other dignitaries had slept, Martha decided it was too big and fancy for her. She took the little bed in the small adjoining room and gave the big bed to Mary Jane.

Despite an accidental fall, which she told no one about, she had a good time. She did not find it particularly overwhelming that her son was in the White House. As Truman observed, "She was just the same Mama she had always been."

Summer 1945

STALIN, CHURCHILL,
AND THE BOMB

O N JULY 6, 1945, after an intensive schedule of meetings, President Truman left the White House by car for Union Station and boarded a special train for Newport News, where the heavy cruiser USS *Augusta* awaited. In company with a single other warship, the cruiser *Philadelphia,* the *Augusta* carried the presidential party through the minefield in Chesapeake Bay and eight days later steamed into the English Channel. There she was met by an escort of British cruisers. Threading minefields and wreck buoys, the *Augusta* ascended the Scheldt estuary, lined with cheering Dutch and Belgians, to Antwerp, where Truman was welcomed by General Eisenhower and a guard picked from the 35th Infantry Division, his old outfit.

The party flew to Potsdam, once the summer home of the Kaisers, and by luck left undamaged. Close to Berlin, it lay in the Russian zone of occupation.

There were three motives behind Truman's decision to arrange the Potsdam Conference. First, there was the multitude of political questions raised among the victorious allies—Poland, the other East European states, the new Italian government, German reparations, many other details of peacemaking.

Second, there was the Pacific war. The savage fighting on Okinawa, with the appearance of the formidable Japanese *kamikaze* suicide planes, made it clear that an invasion of the Japanese home islands would be conducted at frightful cost. Fire-bombing by fleets of giant B-29s was razing one Japanese city after another, but only the optimistic Air Force believed that

En route to Potsdam Conference. The heavy cruiser USS *Augusta* carried Truman to Antwerp, where General Eisenhower came aboard to greet him. During the crossing, the President made himself completely at home, occasionally eating with the crew, watching movies with Secretary of State Byrnes, and exercising on deck each morning.

The Sacred Cow, the President's C-54, was waiting at Antwerp to fly the presidential party to Gatow airfield outside Berlin. There he was met by Secretary of War Stimson and Soviet Ambassadors Gromyko and Gousev.

Truman was the tallest of the Big Three, and to his amusement Churchill and Stalin preferred photos that concealed their stature.

Potsdam Conference opened at five in the afternoon, which seemed to Truman an odd hour to convene. All meetings were held in Cecilienhof Palace, which had been the country estate of former Crown Prince Wilhelm, and was refurnished for the conference. A large paneled room, with a balcony at one end and a round table in the center, was used for the sessions. From left to right are Churchill and the British delegation, Truman (back to camera) and aides, and Stalin and the Soviet delegation.

bombing alone could bring surrender. Former Ambassador Grew thought the Tokyo government might be induced to capitulate if it were given assurance that the Imperial dynasty could be retained. Truman regarded this as a difficult proposition to sell to American public opinion, which had been led to regard Hirohito as hardly different from Hitler. There remained the atomic bomb, but the military chiefs refused to take this seriously in what seemed to be an absence of assurance that it would work.

With diplomatic, military, and scientific problems unresolved, the participation of Soviet Russia in the war against Japan seemed of paramount importance. At Yalta Stalin had promised Roosevelt that Russia would come in not later than three months after V-E Day, or about August 8. This fitted neatly with American military planning, which looked to an invasion of Kyushu in November, followed by an assault on the main Japanese island of Honshu in the spring of 1946. Pinning down Japanese forces in Manchuria was regarded as an important assist which the Russians could deliver.

Third, Truman wished to make personal contact with Churchill and Stalin.

He met Churchill on the morning of July 16, when the celebrated British Prime Minister paid a courtesy call at the "little White House" in Babelsberg, a residential suburb of Potsdam. Truman liked Churchill on sight, though he was unawed. In Truman's view, the U.S. presidency itself provided ample stature for any man. As far as stature went, Truman was amused to note that both Churchill and Stalin were shorter than he, and stood on the step above him when pictures were taken. The "little man with glasses" was the biggest of the Big Three.

Stalin too impressed him favorably. The Soviet dictator was courteous and good-humored, and had an air of frankness not unlike Truman's own straightforward manner. At the opening of the first session in the Cecilienhof Palace Stalin moved that the American President be made chairman of the conference. Five years after the summer of his political nadir, Harry Truman sat at the pinnacle. There was no higher point in politics on the globe than his chair in the Cecilienhof.

The conference was divided into three panels. One—Truman's idea— was of the foreign ministers. Another, to be convened a few days after the opening, was of the military chiefs, to discuss Russian participation in

Henry L. Stimson, right, Roosevelt's Secretary of War, gave Truman a tardy briefing on the atomic bomb, after the new President was sworn in. Earlier, when the Truman Committee began to look into the Manhattan Project, Stimson urgently requested Senator Truman to call off his investigators, giving his word that national security was at stake. Truman acceded, and learned nothing of the project until April 17, 1945. Here the President, with Mrs. Stimson looking on, awards Stimson the Distinguished Service Medal.

the war with Japan. The third was the main panel, that of the heads of state. These latter began their sessions at five in the afternoon, which Truman found an odd time to commence a working day, but which seemed congenial to Churchill and Stalin.

The discussions covering recognition of the former enemy states, German reparations and Poland were generally cordial, but the stubbornness with which Stalin maintained his positions sometimes stirred Churchill or Truman to a show of anger. Particularly troublesome were two matters, of very different weight. The first was Poland, the second Russian demands for massive reparations from Germany. In the case of Poland, the question was no longer the composition of the new Polish government, on which Britain and the U.S. had exhausted their diplomatic resources. It was evident that Stalin's determination to have a "friendly government" in Warsaw was inflexible and backed by a position of power—the Russian army occupied the country. Now the Polish question had shifted to geography. The old Polish state of 1920–39 had been created principally out of former Russian territory. At Yalta Stalin had accepted the "Curzon Line"—a frontier drawn by a League of Nations commission in 1920 but never accepted by the Poles, based on the best ethnic division that could be calculated. But since this involved a large loss of territory by Poland on its eastern frontier, Stalin proposed to compensate the Poles at the expense of Germany. For Poland's western frontier he proposed the Oder and western Neisse Rivers, giving Poland coal-rich Silesia, which Frederick the Great had filched for Prussia two hundred years earlier. Churchill was bitterly opposed to ceding important German territory.

Truman also opposed it, largely because it threatened to complicate the task of feeding the Germans by robbing them of farmland. Related to this was Russia's demand for $10,000,000,000 in reparations. Truman was determined that no arrangement be set up that would result in American aid being funneled into Europe through one door to replace what the Russians were taking out through the other. Within two years Truman would have a much more sophisticated concept of the aid question.

In the end Byrnes worked out a swap—Russian reparations were scaled down and the U.S. agreed to Polish administration of Silesia pending a peace treaty, which amounted to recognition of the change Stalin had made in the map of Central Europe. In a lesser swap, Russia agreed to recognize the new pro-Western government of Italy, and the U.S. and Britain agreed to recognize the Communist-dominated regimes in the East European states.

These solutions were less horse trades than mutual recognitions of the inevitable. A pet project of his own which Truman brought up—internationalization of major European waterways—was doomed for the very reason that there was nothing inevitable about it. In fact it was too new and sweeping an idea to be readily absorbed into discussion. Stalin's interest in waterways was limited to the Black Sea Straits, where he wanted to fulfill an ancient Russian ambition by gaining military control. Molotov cited historical precedent, but history experts Truman and Churchill had to beg off discussion until they could have somebody look up the history.

Despite bickerings, the political sessions of the conference were quite successful. The troubles that soon began arising were the result of arrangements already made before Potsdam, and of the deeper causes inherent in the emerging rivalry of Russia and the U.S.

The military sessions were even more successful. Soviet General Alexei Antonoff defined the Russian military objective in the Far East as destruction of the Japanese forces in Manchuria and occupation of the Liaotung Peninsula. These natural Russian objectives also neatly fitted American strategic thinking.

But under the surface of all the negotiations lurked a strange and sinister secret. On the evening of the day of the military discussions Truman dropped a "casual remark" to Stalin. He mentioned that the U.S. had developed a new weapon of enormous destructive power. Stalin, equally nonchalant, expressed satisfaction and said he hoped it would be used with good effect against the Japanese.

It was one of the least casual "casual remarks" ever dropped. For months, going back long before Truman's presidency, scientists and others in the know had debated the question of secrecy. There were two distinct secrets. The first was the fact that the U.S. was producing atomic bombs. This obviously had to be kept from the Germans and Japanese. Should it also be kept from the Russians? How long could it be? The second secret, the know-how of manufacturing, might better be described as a library of secrets. One of the dilemmas here was stated by scientific adviser Vannevar Bush: "We cannot keep scientific secrets from Russia without also keeping them from the major portion of American scientists." Though few knew it, a great deal of information was already leaking. Many of the top scientists involved in the Manhattan Project were European, including many from

The uranium bomb was test-fired for the first time at Alamogordo, New Mexico, on July 16, the day the Potsdam Conference opened. An extremely graphic report of the effects was forwarded swiftly to Truman, who showed the report to Churchill and dropped a "casual remark" to Stalin.

The two atomic bombs: Slim uranium bomb, ABOVE, was code-named "Thin Man" for Roosevelt, blimp-shaped plutonium "Fat Man" for Churchill. "Thin Man" was credited with only power of a thousand tons of TNT, but tests at Alamogordo revealed that the uranium bomb actually had explosive force of 10,000–20,000 tons of TNT, as did the plutonium bomb.

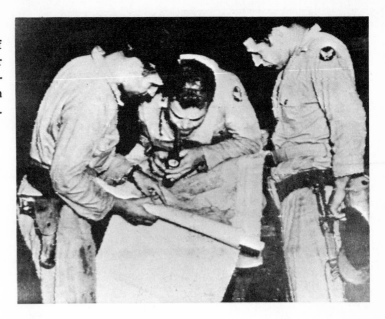

Target Nagasaki. Crew members of Superfortress "No. 77" check their map before taking off. Captain Van-irk, navigator, left, had also flown n the *Enola Gay* three days before.

Hiroshima. The uranium bomb was exploded over the center of the city on August 6 by the B-29 bomber *Enola Gay*. Truman received the news aboard the *Augusta* en route home. His statement to the world declared that "The force from which the sun draws its power has been loosed against those who brought war to the Far East."

areas formerly under German and now under Russian domination. Some might have kept or renewed contact with European colleagues. There were also scientists outside the project, like Niels Bohr of Denmark and Joliot-Curie of France, who knew all about it and had their own views on what should be told the Russians. A British team sent over to learn about the important gaseous-diffusion process contained so many non-British scientists that the Americans joked, "The British delegation doesn't speak English." It was later revealed that one "British" scientist, anti-Nazi German Klaus Fuchs, was at this very moment engaged in methodically transmitting information to Russia from Los Alamos. A more British British scientist, Allan Nunn May, had given uranium samples to the Russian military attaché in Montreal. Doubtless other sources were feeding the Russian espionage network at first or second hand. Bohr, who had been invited to work in Russia, thought the Russians knew what the Americans were up to as early as 1943.

Thus Truman's "casual remark" could not have totally amazed Stalin. Just as straightforward Harry Truman could dissemble, so could frank Joe Stalin. Possibly, Stalin did not attach great importance to the matter for the same reason that most of the American military did not. Until it actually exploded, it was difficult for a non-scientist to take the bomb seriously.

Truman's own inadequate briefing left him insufficiently aware of one important aspect of the new weapon. This was the fact that the Manhattan Project was producing not one, but two very different types of bombs. One contained uranium, the other plutonium. The two did not even look alike, and the difference between them was significant. The decision to give Stalin an inkling had been reached as a result of a test at Alamogordo, New Mexico, a few days earlier. Stimson had flown to Potsdam with a graphic report, which Truman had promptly shown to Churchill.

But the Alamogordo test was of the uranium bomb. The plutonium device, also in an advanced stage of preparation, required no testing. The scientists were certain that it would go off. Further, it was to the plutonium bomb that Groves and the scientists pinned their chief hopes. Their expectations for the uranium bomb were at best the equivalent of a thousand tons of TNT, whereas they credited the plutonium bomb with a force of 10,000 tons. This ambiguity may also have contributed to Truman's view of the bomb. Had it no more than fulfilled expectations, the uranium

A-bomb would have been less than the equivalent of a B-29 raid.

The surprising power—10,000–20,000 tons—and sudden reality, of the uranium bomb, forced Truman to consider discussion with Stalin. Churchill, who wished maximum information to be given the British, wanted minimum for the Russians. The result was the "casual remark."

There was another question. Even more important than what to tell the Russians was what to do to the Japanese. Should the bomb be dropped on a Japanese city? Or should it be exploded over an empty area of Japan as a demonstration? How much should the Japanese be told in advance about it? This last was doubly important, for it also included the question of how much the world—and the American people—should be told.

The Japanese were known to be looking for a way out of the war. Three days before Potsdam American intelligence began reading code messages from Tokyo to the Japanese Ambassador to Moscow that made this unmistakable.

Foremost in Truman's mind was the terrible blood bath that awaited American soldiers should the scheduled invasion of the Japanese home islands be carried out. The news from Alamogordo opened the prospect of inducing a Japanese surrender.

It was this prospect, rather than his dealings with Stalin, as Churchill mistakenly imagined, that accounted for Truman's jubilation at Potsdam. His preoccupation with the military problem of the invasion of Japan may even have blinded him to the possibility of not using the bomb at all, or of restricting its use to a demonstration on Japanese soil. Such restraint would have permitted America to escape the onus of introducing the frightful new weapon, and strengthened the U.S. moral position in the postwar world. Had the Potsdam Declaration, issued on July 26, been framed with this in mind, it might have given the Japanese—and the world—a more precise clue to what was coming. Instead it accompanied a summons to the Japanese to surrender with nothing more than a general threat of destruction.

In the immediate aftermath, far more attention was given to the question of whether the bomb could have been used to "keep the Russians out of the Pacific war" than to whether it might not have been used at all. Had the bomb—either the uranium or the plutonium variety—been ready a couple of months earlier, the war might have been ended before the Russian army was ready to move. However, Stalin's aims in entering the

Surrender of Japan. ABOVE, Japanese plenipotentiaries were received aboard the battleship *Missouri* by General MacArthur, Allied Supreme Commander, in a solemn ceremony. At home in the U.S. downtowns were jammed (scene is Times Square, New
York) with crowds delirious over final end of war. But in Manchuria a new war was
already preparing. Japanese machine guns, RIGHT, surrendered to Russian armies invad-
ing Manchuria, ended up in the hands of Chinese Communists, who used them effectively
in the civil war that broke out between Nationalists and Communists for control of the
world's largest country.

war did not actually conflict with America's. What Stalin wanted to do was to recover the losses Russia had suffered in the Russo-Japanese War of 1904–5, and it would have been difficult for Truman to offer good reasons why he should not. With the bomb scheduled to become operational at the very date of the projected Russian entry, the idea of using it to "keep the Russians out" was far-fetched.

The conservative military approach which Truman adopted restricted discussion of the bomb to the scientists and military men. The public, both American and world, learned what was afoot for the first time on August 6, shortly after the Japanese learned the stunning news that a sizable Japanese city, Hiroshima, had been largely wiped out by a single bomb.

Truman, lunching with the sailors aboard the homeward-bound *Augusta,* received a radio message from Stimson shortly before the release of the news, with the information, "First reports indicate complete success."

One effect of the shattering news was to move the Japanese government, torn between bloody bitter-enders and despairing peace-wishers, toward an acceptance of the Potsdam Declaration. Another was to nudge Stalin into a swifter entry. The Russian declaration of war was accompanied by a massive invasion of Manchuria against much weaker Japanese forces than had been foreseen by either Russian or American military planners.

Before the Japanese government could recover from the double blow of Hiroshima and Russian entry into the war, a second bomb—the untested plutonium type—was dropped on the city of Nagasaki. As the scientists had predicted, it went off. The purpose of the quick follow-up, in General Groves' words, was "so that the Japanese would not have time to recover their balance."

General Groves' calculation was sound. Early on the morning of August 10, the day after Nagasaki, Emperor Hirohito broke the deadlock in the Tokyo cabinet by directing acceptance of the Potsdam Declaration as a basis for peace. The Japanese reply included "the understanding that the said declaration does not comprise any demand which prejudices the prerogatives of His Majesty as a Sovereign Ruler." Transmitted via Sweden and Switzerland, the Japanese note caused some discussion in Washington because of the proviso in favor of the Emperor, but there was little doubt that it signified the end of the war. Truman ordered cessation of atomic bombing, and fissionable material for the third bomb, about to be shipped to Tinian for assembly, was held up.

Precedent-shattering meeting between General Douglas MacArthur, Supreme Commander in Japan, and Japanese Emperor Hirohito was held in October, 1945, just a month after the Japanese surrender. General MacArthur was a successful administrator, helping Japan move toward a stable democratic form of government while still retaining the Emperor.

A reply was drafted which implied, without quite specifying, that the Emperor could be retained. A provision requiring that Hirohito himself sign the instrument of surrender was wisely stricken at the suggestion of the British, who had a finer sensitivity than Truman and Byrnes to the feelings of royalty.

On the other hand, steps were taken to make the surrender ceremony in Tokyo Bay as impressive as possible. Truman sentimentally chose the new battleship *Missouri,* which his daughter Margaret had christened, for the reception of the Japanese plenipotentiaries by General Douglas MacArthur, Allied Supreme Commander. Truman listened along with the rest of America to the radio account, and then, when the announcer in Tokyo Bay switched to the White House, addressed the nation, proclaiming the following day, Sunday, September 2, as V-J Day.

The announcement was anticlimactic; the war had really ended two weeks earlier. Its lightning-like dénouement had terminated the first stage of Truman's presidency, which had lasted just over four months. Few four-month periods since the Republic's beginnings have been so crowded with history.

1945–1948

PROSPERITY AND COLD WAR

IN HIS cabin aboard the *Augusta* en route home Truman finished work on the report which he planned to deliver to Congress and the people. At his side was Judge Samuel I. Rosenman, one of FDR's chief aides, whom Truman had taken along to Potsdam.

"Sam," the President said as they finished, "one of the first things I want to do after we get home is to get busy on my domestic program." He did not want to wait till January when his State of the Union message would be due, but planned to deliver as soon as possible a statement of the direction in which he felt the U.S. should go in the coming years. Rosenman listened with growing enthusiasm. "Mr. President," he said, "this is the most exciting and pleasant surprise I have had in a long time."

Rosenman confessed that he had been listening too much to rumors about Truman's intentions, especially some put out by Truman's more conservative friends, whose wish was father to the thought that now with Truman in the White House, New Deal liberalism was finished. As Rosenman observed, to vote for a liberal program in Congress was one thing, but to propose it as head of a party and a government something else.

Rosenman went to work on a draft of Truman's ideas. Back in Washington Truman edited the draft, then had it printed in galleys and gone over by his top advisers, who now included a bright Washington lawyer named Clark Clifford. The revised galleys were printed and distributed to all Cabinet members and heads of federal agencies. The final version, 16,000 words long, was not delivered as a speech, but was distributed to all members of Congress and read by the clerks of the two Houses.

Central Park, New York, was jammed with close to two million persons on Navy Day, October 27, 1945, when President Truman made his first official trip to New York and delivered a major foreign-policy address. Earlier in the day he had christened the new aircraft carrier *Franklin D. Roosevelt* and paid a visit to Fleet Admiral William Leahy, his chief of staff, aboard the battleship *Missouri,* BELOW. From left are Admiral Jonas H. Ingram, Admiral Leahy, the President, and Brigadier General Harry H. Vaughan.

Truman and top congressional leaders met shortly after V-J Day to go over the domestic problems of shifting from a wartime to a peacetime economy. From left are Speaker of the House Sam Rayburn, the President, Senate Majority Leader Alben Barkley, and Senator Kenneth McKellar, President Pro Tempore of the Senate.

Prime Minister Attlee came to Washington in the fall of 1945 partly to discuss problems of atomic energy (Britain wanted maximum access to our atomic secrets) and partly to confer with the President on problems growing out of the termination of Lend-Lease (Britain wanted a whopping loan). Truman approved sharing secrets, with safeguards, and a loan at a tougher rate than Attlee had asked.

The main emphasis was on reconversion from war to peace. Truman
sought an orderly change-over with safeguards against runaway inflation or
paralyzing deflation. The country's economic situation was basically strong,
with an expanded industrial capacity ready to turn out goods and with
large war-enforced savings in the hands of consumers. The problem was
how to keep things in balance while the industrial machine shifted gears.
Despite the message's focus on the immediate emergency, many recommendations had an unmistakably New Dealish tinge, such as an increase in
the minimum wage and a call for federal housing. Through the fall additional messages spelled out further liberal reforms: aid to education, what
later became medicare, nationalization of atomic energy, the St. Lawrence
Seaway. The whole added up to a program of 14-karat liberalism that
Truman called the "Fair Deal"—a name which underlined its character as
a continuation of FDR's New Deal.

As such, it came under immediate fire from conservatives in and out
of Congress. Paradoxically, however, the long-range reforms stirred less
controversy than the short-range reconversion measures. Essentially, the
trouble was that while nobody wanted inflation, every business and industry
wanted freedom from wartime price controls. Lobbyists and congressmen
serving special-interest blocs wrangled tenaciously for their clients, and
though labor and some consumers' groups rallied to Truman's support, the
general public did not understand the issue clearly enough.

Controls on wages, prices, and rents were due to expire six months
after V-J Day. Congress reluctantly extended them a little longer, to June
30, 1946, and then passed a bill renewing the life of the Office of Price
Administration but with such feeble powers that Truman vetoed the bill,
feeling its passage would merely confuse people further. Prices, especially
meat prices, shot up.

The pressure against price control came from business. It was accompanied
by a corresponding pressure from labor against wage control. War-production
overtime pay had in effect raised wages despite the freeze on hourly pay;
reconversion, by knocking out the overtime, brought widespread wage cuts.
At the same time such labor leaders as Walter Reuther pointed to high
profits in industry as a basis for granting substantial pay increases without
raising prices. The year 1946 was consequently filled with strike headlines,
which added to the general sense of irritation.

In May two labor crises boiled up to the White House summit. One, in the perennially embattled coal mines, seemed to be ended by a presidential seizure order followed by a compromise settlement. The other, involving the railroads, brought a dramatic personal confrontation. A presidential compromise proposal was accepted by eighteen of the twenty operating unions but rejected by the two most important—the engineers and the trainmen. Three White House conferences with A. F. Whitney and Alvanley Johnston, presidents of the recalcitrant unions, brought no solution. What they did instead was to ignite the Truman temper. When the two veteran labor leaders reiterated their intention to strike the nation's railways he informed them, "You are not going to tie up the country. If this is the way you want it, we'll stop you." He did. First he delivered a blistering radio attack (though considerably watered down from his first hot-headed draft). Next he went to Congress with a speech asking for an extremely drastic anti-strike law, giving the President power to draft strikers into the armed forces. He was halfway through the speech when Leslie Biffle, secretary of the Senate, handed him a note announcing that the rail strike had been settled.

Late in the year John L. Lewis, the powerful and picturesque head of the United Mine Workers, capriciously found fault with the contract he had signed in May and threatened a strike. The mines were still under government seizure. At Truman's direction the Justice Department successfully sought an injunction to restrain Lewis. When Lewis refused to comply with the injunction he was cited for contempt and fined $10,000 personally, while his union was fined a record $3,500,000. Lewis backed down by appealing the judgment to the Supreme Court and then canceling the strike while the Court deliberated. The Court's decision sustained the injunction, though the fine against the union was reduced to $700,000.

The House passed Truman's proposed anti-strike bill at once, but the Senate, under less direct public pressure, deliberated and eventually killed it. Already in June Truman had vetoed a tough anti-strike bill passed by Congress which now went back to work on a complicated set of provisions, eventually to become the Taft-Hartley law. Truman vetoed that, but Congress passed it over his veto, in the face of angry opposition from labor. The merits and defects of Taft-Hartley proved less than either side believed but the issue remained politically hot for years to come. The November 1946 congressional elections were a disaster for the Democrats, and the law was the achievement of the new Republican-dominated 80th Congress.

By the time the new Congress opened for business some of the spotlight had switched from labor disturbances and price control to foreign affairs and especially to the suddenly alarming China question. During the war a section of largely conservative U.S. opinion had held that China and the Pacific theatre were being neglected by an administration too preoccupied with Europe.

Now the growing friction with Soviet Russia was again attracting most of the State Department's attention to Europe. In March of 1946 Winston Churchill made the keynote speech of the Cold War at Fulton, Missouri. Churchill, now out of power, was recruited to address the graduating class of little Westminster College, alma mater of Harry Vaughan, by Vaughan's friend Harry Truman. "From Stettin in the Baltic to Trieste in the Adriatic, an iron curtain has descended across the continent," said Churchill. "Behind that line lie all the capitals of the ancient states of central and eastern Europe . . . all these famous cities and the populations around them . . . are subject . . . to a very high and increasing measure of control from Moscow. Athens alone, with its immortal glories, is free to decide its future at an election under British, American and French observation." Further, Churchill asserted, "the Communist parties, or fifth column, constitute a growing challenge and peril to Christian civilization," in the West European states.

The speech had tremendous impact in the U.S., where its vivid image of a divided and hostile world polarized between Russia and the U.S. was widely accepted as the basis for future American policy. Only a few voices expressed doubts. One of these was in Truman's Cabinet. It belonged to Henry A. Wallace, the man Truman had replaced as Vice-President, and whom Roosevelt had made Secretary of Commerce in his last month in office. Wallace sought to persuade Truman that friendship with Russia was possible, and that an attempt should be made to alleviate Russian fears of a new "capitalist encirclement." When in September Wallace reiterated his views in a speech in Madison Square Garden Truman found himself in an embarrassing dilemma. His first reaction when queried by newsmen was to put his foot in his mouth by saying Wallace's speech corresponded to administration policy. This brought sharp reactions from Congress and especially from Secretary of State Byrnes. Truman finally extricated himself by firing Wallace.

But Wallace, like Byrnes and Truman, was primarily preoccupied with

Americans had money and wanted to spend it. New cars were hot off the assembly line; nylon stockings were available; more new homes were going up than ever before, but nothing could keep pace with the insistent consumer demand for these and other goods. And over strong opposition from the President, the Office of Price Administration was wrecked in 1946, bringing about inflation and heavy shortages. In 1947, BELOW, the President appealed to merchants to help curb inflation by lowering prices.

Former President Herbert Hoover twice served important missions for Truman, first as chairman of the Famine Emergency Commission in 1946, later as chairman of the Hoover Commission on government reorganization, which produced a constructive plan for streamlining the government.

The "Marshall Plan," named for Truman's Secretary of State, former commanding general George C. Marshall, was phenomenally successful in promoting European recovery. Ridiculed in some quarters as a waste of money, the Marshall Plan helped Western Europe rebuild its war-shattered economy in amazingly quick time. Within a few years European production was soaring above prewar level, enabling Europe to contribute to healthy world trade and to aid developing countries.

Europe. None of them foresaw the dramatic turn events were about to take in Asia. These events, over the next two years, hardened the "China bloc" into a resentful and suspicious group of congressmen and editors who wielded considerable power. Their essential thesis was that the Nationalist government of Chiang Kai-shek had been betrayed by stupidity, and/or treason, inside the U.S. government.

The truth was that the ratio of strength between the Nationalists and Communists in China had been concealed from the world by the success of Chiang Kai-shek in maintaining himself against the Japanese. The difficulties experienced by the Japanese army in China were actually more geographical than military, and the façade of Chiang's power was highly misleading.

Despite lengthy and hazardous supply routes, enough U.S. military aid had gone to Chiang to make him, on paper, master of China after the Japanese surrender. Chiang apparently thought so himself, though his statement of what he required in the way of a military establishment to insure "political stability" was rather startling—ninety divisions, including thirty equipped like U.S. divisions. But from the moment of Japanese surrender it became evident that Chiang had great trouble moving his armies about China, and worse, that the armies were not reliable. Thanks to strenuous American efforts in airlifting Nationalist troops, in temporarily occupying ports till the Nationalists could reach them, and even in enlisting Japanese garrisons to hold points against capture by the Communists, Chiang was able to occupy most of the large cities. Byrnes found himself in the odd position of having to explain to a politely inquisitive Stalin why American troops were remaining in China so long. But with the Communists in control of most of the countryside it already looked as if the only alternative to civil war was the formation of a government including both Communists and Nationalists. To get such a broad-based government organized was the mission Truman entrusted to General George C. Marshall, the distinguished wartime chief of staff. Marshall ran into insuperable problems, in which Chiang appeared to play the most obstructive role. Over Marshall's warnings, Chiang ultimately challenged the Communists to fight it out. After a few opening successes the Nationalists suffered a series of defeats which were the more decisive for being ingloriously bloodless. Chiang's troops and generals refused to fight for him, and passed over in large numbers to the enemy, taking with them their American equipment.

By that time the Truman administration had more than atoned for whatever shortness of vision it displayed in Asia by two landmark strokes of policy in Europe. The decision to employ American economic power to protect non-Communist nations from Communist pressure, recommended by Churchill and supported by George Kennan, a scholarly Russian expert in the State Department, found expression in what came to be known as the "Truman Doctrine." Churchill had made a deal with Stalin in the autumn of 1944 by which Greece and Turkey were recognized as being of special importance to Britain. But the military support required by the Greeks and Turks was becoming more than Britain could supply. Greece was in a state of civil war, and Turkey was still desperately resisting Soviet diplomatic pressure on the Straits issue. Truman agreed to take over the British commitment, and Congress went along, voting generous military aid. The move worked. Turkey kept the Straits in her own hands and the anti-Communists won the civil war in Greece.

In a parallel development, American firmness had already forced the Russians to withdraw from Iran, where Stalin had sought to take advantage of a temporary wartime arrangement to win permanent Russian influence.

Even more important than the Truman Doctrine was the Marshall Plan, one of the most farsighted and eminently successful foreign policy ventures in U.S. history. Despite American aid in many forms, the European countries were barely holding their own economically, with little headway toward real recovery from the war. America, on the other hand, was riding a powerful wave of postwar prosperity. A question arose among economists— how long could America enjoy economic well-being when the important West European market remained depressed? The basic difficulty in Europe was lack of investment capital to rebuild the region's damaged and neglected industrial plant.

The necessary capital could only come, in one form or another, from the U.S. The question of how a program of such fundamental economic assistance could best be formulated occupied Truman, his new Secretary of State Marshall, and several subordinates in the spring of 1947. In May Truman was invited to give a speech at the Mississippi Delta Council's meeting. Because the vote on the Greece-Turkey aid bill was coming up he sent in his place Undersecretary of State Dean Acheson. Although Acheson's speech detailing Europe's needs and America's responsibility stirred the interest of his farm audience, it received little attention in the big-city press. But the

Hideki Tojo, right, Japanese premier through most of World War II, was the most prominent of twenty-five defendants in the war crimes trials held in Tokyo in December 1947. He was sworn in by Captain D. S. Van Meter.

Generalissimo Chiang Kai-shek, BELOW, shown reading his own book, *China's Destiny,* grossly underestimated the strength of his adversary, Mao Tse-tung.

Civil war in China broke out despite General Marshall's efforts at conciliation. ABOVE, Mao's Communist troops proved much more determined and better led than the Nationalists.

BELOW, Schoolgirls welcome Red troops occupying the city of Canton in early 1950.

The State of Israel was born May 15, 1948, when British withdrawal was swiftly followed by President Truman's recognition of the new nation. Here immigrants from Romania, who had fought side by side with the French resistance against the Germans, get a glimpse at their new homeland from their ship entering Haifa harbor.

John L. Lewis, powerful head of the United Mine Workers, defied Truman by calling a strike of the nation's coal mines while the mines were under government seizure in 1946. Truman promptly accepted the challenge, ordered the Justice Department to get an injunction, and forced Lewis to back down. Both Lewis and the union were given heavy fines. RIGHT, a Pennsylvania miner shows what he thinks of the court ruling. It was largely the coal strike, and a threatened national railroad strike the same year, that spurred Senate Majority Leader Robert A. Taft of Ohio, BELOW, to engineer a strong bill curbing strikes. This bill—the Taft-Hartley Act—was bitterly opposed by labor and passed over Truman's veto in June 1947.

European papers treated it extensively, the London *Times* printing it nearly in full. It became an active subject for discussion abroad, and American commentators also began to take notice of it.

Then on June 5 Secretary Marshall elaborated the idea in a speech at the Harvard commencement. This time the press was alerted, though once more interest in Europe ran way ahead of that in America. The essence of the Acheson-Marshall proposals was that if the European nations got together on an economic recovery program of continental scope, the U.S. would underwrite it. European governments picked up the ball with extraordinary alacrity; on July 12, barely a month after Marshall's speech, the Paris Conference opened.

The Marshall Plan brought cheers from London, Paris, and other West European capitals, but it placed Moscow in an acute dilemma. Apparently Stalin's first decision was to join and get some of the proffered aid for Russia and her satellites. Molotov came to Paris at the head of a delegation. But after a few days the Russians suddenly withdrew, denouncing the whole scheme as an American capitalist plot. Under naked Russian pressure, the satellites had to withdraw too.

It was a bad blunder on Stalin's part. Truman had taken precautions to assure bipartisan support in Congress, but whether any Congress, let alone a Republican-dominated one, would have voted billions of dollars in aid to Communist and non-Communist countries alike must certainly be classed as doubtful. The Marshall Plan was not designed to hurt Communism, but to help European recovery. The withdrawal of Russia from the Paris Conference insured that it would do both.

Sixteen nations remained: Britain, France, Belgium, the Netherlands, Luxembourg, Denmark, Norway, Greece, Iceland, Austria, Italy, Ireland, Portugal, Sweden, Switzerland, and Turkey. Not all had suffered war damage, or even fought in the war. But the participation of the broadest possible group provided the basis for efficient, long-range planning. Later on, the important addition of West Germany was made.

What the conference came up with was a four-year plan to boost European productivity back to and above prewar levels. In the detailed blueprint which the Europeans submitted to Washington in astonishingly swift time they asked for $22,000,000,000 over the years 1948–52. Ultimately they got a little more than half that—and it was enough to do the job. The money was used to excellent effect, thanks not only to the unified sixteen-nation approach, but also because the Marshall Plan amounted to a "psychological blood transfusion." The tremendously hopeful atmosphere it suddenly generated supplied momentum for advance. Currencies were stabilized, agricultural production steadily increased, and as Europeans ate better and felt more secure, industrial production rose spectacularly. Three years after the program began, production had leaped 49 percent over prewar levels. U. S.-European trade was soon booming.

Truman took a number of measures to overcome congressional opposition, including sending an eighteen-member bi-partisan delegation of Senators and Representatives to Europe to make their own independent study. But the Marshall Plan would still have run into strong opposition except for a new and dramatic event in Europe. Early in 1948 the Czechoslovakian Communists, heretofore a strong minority in the Prague government, staged a *coup d'état*. Congress's initial appropriation for Western European recovery seemed almost an American answer to the Czech coup.

Yet courageous and imaginative though the Marshall Plan was, it did not inspire much applause in the United States. Conservatives sniped at it ("Operation Rathole" said the *New York Daily News*) and liberals defended it as an unfortunate necessity.

Even some liberals attacked it. On December 29, 1947, Henry Wallace made an impassioned radio address announcing the formation of a third party dedicated to peace with Russia.

Wallace's move raised a disturbing specter for Truman and the Democrats —the La Follette Progressive defection of 1924, which had resulted in an electoral debacle for the Democrats. Nor was Wallace the only problem. After three years in the White House Harry Truman enjoyed so little popularity that even his friends were urging him not to run for re-election.

1948

THE UPSET OF THE CENTURY

AT FIRST blush Truman's desperate political plight of 1948 appears surprising. He had grappled manfully with extremely difficult problems, and not without success. His mistakes were minor in comparison with his impressive demonstrations of courage, patriotism and liberalism.

The political atmosphere of 1948 seems even more puzzling in the context of the economic situation. Forebodings of experts to the contrary, the war boom carried right into the election year. Americans had never before eaten or drunk so well, driven so many or such large automobiles, lived in or owned such comfortable houses. They had never done so much vacation traveling, read so many books, or worn such expensive clothes. By the standard indicators of how good everybody had it, Truman and the Democrats should have been odds-on favorites.

Instead, in the spring of 1948 the popularity of Truman and the Democrats stood so low that it was manifest to every Washington correspondent, newspaper editor, columnist, and commentator that the next President would inevitably be a Republican.

In addition to the revolt of Wallace and the left-wing liberals, there was a threatening insurrection on the right, by southern conservatives in arms over Truman's strong civil-rights message delivered early in the spring. The China bloc was frustrated by the successes the Communists were scoring in the Chinese civil war. Early stirrings of the "loyalty" panic soon to sweep Washington and the nation gave credibility to the charge that Truman was "soft on Communism."

More important than any of these controversies among moderate, middle-of-the-road Americans were two large, cloudy, but boiling-hot domestic issues: strikes and inflation. Industrial unionism was still a new and unpopular element in American life, and most ordinary people considered a strike, any strike, necessarily bad. Many thought strikes should not be permitted. Despite Truman's toughness with John L. Lewis and the railroad brotherhoods, he was regarded as soft on unions because of his opposition to the Taft-Hartley Act. The exceptional number of strikes in the postwar period was an inevitable result of postwar economics, and in any case did no discernible harm—production went steadily up.

In his Taft-Hartley veto, Truman had accurately identified the "erroneous assumptions . . . that strikes are called in haste as the result of inflamed passions, and that union leaders do not represent the wishes of the workers." These wrong assumptions remained widespread, and hurt Truman.

The other major domestic issue, inflation, was even more alarming to most people. The fact that prices had doubled since 1939 seemed a self-evident catastrophe except to professional economists. That the price rise was a symptom of a healthy, booming economy, with full employment and high wages, was a truth not at all grasped by the general public, or even the educated elite. The specter of "runaway inflation" wiping out everyone's savings reinforced an ancient conservative faith in "the soundness of the dollar." The "New Economics" with its emphasis on gross national product and rate of growth was still several years in the future. A magazine which polled leading newspaper editors on what the nation's "goals" should be found that an overwhelming majority thought the No. 1 goal should be to halt inflation. To judge from some of the things written by editors during the Truman administration one would have imagined America teetering on the brink of economic disaster rather than emerging triumphantly from it. And Truman, despite his strong losing fight for price control, was somehow blamed. As a final irony, the steep price rise of the past seven years had just been halted, though no one knew it yet.

All these elements of mistrust, anger, and fear merged in a general feeling that the Democrats had been in too long. Any political party that commands power for sixteen years is in trouble, and the Republican victories in the 1946 congressional elections had seemed an unmistakable harbinger of change.

Democratic leaders were as certain as Republicans that Truman could not win. They were certain, in fact, that no Democrat could win, and from one end of the country to the other they panicked. Their panic took the form of a headlong pursuit of a will-o'-the-wisp—General Dwight D. Eisenhower, a universally popular military figure whose politics possessed the rare charm of being totally invisible. Despite a severely negative silence from Eisenhower, Democratic bosses—Hague of New Jersey, Arvey of Chicago, Bailey of Connecticut and many more—joined such liberals as Hubert Humphrey, James and Elliott Roosevelt, Paul Douglas, Chester Bowles in an undignified courtship, carried on almost to the eve of the Democratic convention.

Truman himself is said to have had some early impulses toward embracing Eisenhower as a Democratic candidate. If so, the unseemly Eisenhower boom among Democratic senators, congressmen, governors, financial chairmen, and committeemen, which amounted to a massive slap in Truman's face, sufficed to make up his mind in the opposite direction. As President, he knew he could control the convention's choice no matter what anybody else thought, and on March 8, 1948, he announced his intention of running.

He heard promptly from all the columnists, editors, and other pundits, not to mention his own friends. He couldn't win. He was a sure loser. He had no chance. But Harry Truman had heard that song before. It had not stopped him before and it did not stop him now.

At his press conference the sophisticated and tolerant correspondents asked him if he thought he could get re-elected. He said yes. What about the Gallup poll, which showed that only 36 percent of the voters approved of his administration? Truman said the people had been misled about a number of things and did not yet understand the issues in the coming election. The skeptical reporters asked him how the people were going to get to understand the issues, and Truman answered that when he got finished explaining the issues the people would understand them. Nobody bought a word of that.

There were two oversights in the experts' appraisal of Truman. They did not sufficiently recognize the genuine quality of his liberalism, and they did not fully appreciate his political adroitness. Some saw him as not only a sure loser, but even as a dog in the manger wrecking the Democrats' only chance of winning—via Eisenhower. Looking back on that strange election year, it seems as if almost everyone was crazy except Truman.

Late in the spring he resolved on a bold move to infuse courage into his own followers. Seizing the opportunity presented by an invitation from

Truman accepts the nomination: Against the advice of columnists, editorial writers, friends and enemies who were certain he could not win, Truman decided to run for re-election. His fighting acceptance speech, delivered at two in the morning, electrified a torpid Democratic convention.

Governor Thomas E. Dewey of New York, the Republican nominee, was assured of victory by the press and the polls. Suave, polished, a good speaker with an impressive record in public life, Dewey made a formidable antagonist.

Dixiecrat walkout followed adoption of Truman's strong civil-rights message to Congress as part of the Democratic platform. The revolt cost Truman the electoral votes of four southern states.

Left-wing Progressive Party, launched by Henry Wallace, nominated Wallace for President and Senator Glen Taylor of Idaho, left, for Vice-President. Wallace, who opposed Truman's tough anti-Russian stand, threatened to take enough votes in the big cities to swing several important states to the Republicans.

the University of California to deliver the commencement address, he set out on a cross-country speaking tour. Though the trip was brazenly labeled non-political and charged to presidential travel expenses—the Democratic party treasury was empty—its real character was scarcely disguised. The presidential train made stops from Washington to the Coast, and at each stop Truman appeared on the observation platform to talk. His speeches were in a new style. He had never felt at home delivering set-piece orations in the Senate and elsewhere, and now he simply leaned over the rail and, as one reporter put it, talked to the people as if he were leaning over the back fence. He threw quips and barbs at the Republicans in Congress, and said that the Democrats who had stayed home on Election Day in 1946 got exactly what they deserved—"that do-nothing Republican Eightieth Congress." The crowd relished his down-to-earth informality and cheered his honest partisan politics. Sometimes the talk was two-way. A man shouted, "Lay it on, Harry! Give 'em hell!" Truman turned to his enthusiastic interlocutor and told him person-to-person, "I intend to!"

Margaret and Bess, who were home in Independence when the trip started, came aboard in Omaha. In the cities, where the train was abandoned for a motorcade, the people were lined up "fifty deep," according to Margaret. "They were on the roofs of barns and filling stations. Lots of them had brought their children and they held them up to see Dad. There was something immensely touching and encouraging about the personal way they took him to their hearts."

The Republicans were justifiably outraged. Senator Robert A. Taft protested that Truman was "blackguarding Congress at whistlestops all across the country," a slip on which Truman's people promptly capitalized. They wired the mayors of the towns and cities through which the Truman train was passing and asked if they agreed with Senator Taft's description of their towns as "whistlestops." The negative and often sarcastic responses made good copy for the press and helped cancel out Taft's legitimate complaint. The incident put the word "whistlestop" in the political vocabulary and forever memorialized the 1948 campaign.

Both parties held their conventions in Philadelphia, the Republicans in June, the Democrats in July. Confidence in victory made the Republican nomination an eagerly sought prize, but Governor Thomas E. Dewey of New York, the party standard bearer in 1944, fought off his challengers and secured the nomination. Dewey was by now a political veteran, shrewd, thoroughgoing, prudent, fortified by a strong organization and a good record as governor. He had a rich campaign treasury, a tribute to the political axiom that nothing succeeds like the likelihood of success. The press was as usual behind the Republican ticket, and for once confident of victory. Dewey had only one problem, the scars left from the pre-convention battles. To heal the wounds in his party and to avoid antagonizing any doubtful voters, he decided to pitch his campaign on high ground. His speeches, cast from generalities, were designed less to arouse than to soothe. This was sound strategy for a candidate who had only to hold his following to insure easy victory.

In contrast to the congenial optimism reigning in the Republican camp, the Democratic convention was torpid and gloomy. The only two events that gave it any life seemed to presage ill. One was the keynote speech by Senator Barkley, venerable majority leader of the Senate, loaded with the orotund rhetoric of yesteryear. The old-fashioned approach provoked so much nostalgia that the convention picked Barkley as the vice-presidential candidate, thereby handing Truman another liability. A young liberal from another part of the country would have suited Truman better than the septuagenarian senator from Kentucky, a Midwestern border state like Missouri. The second event occurred two days later when Hubert Humphrey led a successful floor fight to write Truman's civil-rights message into the platform. The result was the secession of the "Dixiecrat" bloc headed by Governor J. Strom Thurmond of South Carolina.

Truman had forced integration on the armed services against resistance, particularly from the Navy, and it had worked. This accomplishment made Truman appear a more dangerous President than Roosevelt had been, in the eyes of the southern segregationists. When a reporter suggested to Governor Thurmond that Truman was "only following the platform that Roosevelt advocated," Thurmond answered, "I agree, but Truman really *means* it."

The southern delegates who did not bolt gave their votes to Senator Richard B. Russell of Georgia, but Truman was finally nominated, 947½ to 263. By the time the balloting and demonstrating was over it was nearly two o'clock in the morning. Truman had been waiting for hours on a small balcony overlooking the Pennsylvania Railroad yards. It was insufferably hot, the delegates were worn out, an anticlimax seemed inevitable. Instead Truman brought the crowd to its feet with a rousing opener: "Senator Barkley and I will win this election and make the Republicans like it—don't you forget that!"

The fighting speech that followed stirred storms of applause. Truman pointed to the benefits won by various sections of the population under the New and Fair Deals, and bluntly demanded their votes in return. "Never in the world were the farmers of any country as prosperous as the farmers of the United States, and if they don't do their duty by the Democratic party, they are the most ungrateful people in the world . . . Labor never had but one friend in politics, and that is the Democratic party of Franklin D. Roosevelt. And . . . they are the most ungrateful people in the world if they pass the Democratic party by this year."

Then he sounded what was to be the keynote of the whole campaign— a gloves-off, slam-bang assault on the "Republican Eightieth Congress." He listed its failures in detail and asserted, "The Republican party favors the privileged few and not the common everyday man. Ever since its inception, that party has been under the control of special privilege, and they concretely proved it in the Eightieth Congress . . ."

At the very end of the speech, he released a bombshell he had been saving. "On the twenty-sixth day of July, which out in Missouri we call 'Turnip Day,' I am going to call Congress back and ask them to pass laws to halt rising prices, to meet the housing crisis—which they are saying they are for in their platform.

"At the same time I shall ask them to act upon other vitally needed measures, such as aid to education, which they say they are for; a national health program; civil-rights legislation, which they say they are for; an increase in the minimum wage, which I doubt very much they are for [loud laughter at that point]; extension of the Social Security coverage and increased benefits, which they say they are for; funds for projects needed in our program to provide public power and cheap electricity. By indirection, this Eightieth Congress has tried to sabotage the power policies the United States has pursued for fourteen years. That power lobby is as bad as the real-estate lobby which is sitting on the housing bill.

"I shall ask for adequate and decent laws for displaced persons in place of this anti-Semitic, anti-Catholic law which this Eightieth Congress passed [The Displaced Persons Act of 1948] . . .

"Now, my friends, if there is any reality behind that Republican platform, we ought to get some action from a short session of the Eightieth Congress.

They can do this job in fifteen days, if they want to do it. They will still have time to go out and run for office.

"They are going to try to dodge their responsibility. They are going to drag all the red herrings they can across this campaign, but I am here to say that Senator Barkley and I are not going to let them get away with it."

Congress reconvened in the mood of a wet hen and, as Truman had foreseen, accomplished virtually nothing. Now he had the weapon he needed for his campaign.

That it would be an uphill fight even Truman readily conceded. A revealing crisis developed in the very first round, Truman's kickoff speech in Detroit on Labor Day. Two days before the speech the broadcasting company peremptorily demanded $50,000 cash in advance or no radio broadcast. Oscar Chapman, in charge of arrangements, appealed to the labor leaders in Detroit, but they were unable to raise such a sum on such short notice. Chairman McGrath in New York was equally helpless.

Finally Chapman telephoned his old friend Governor Roy J. Turner of Oklahoma, an oil man with wealthy friends, and told him the problem. Two hours later Turner called back. He had raised the money. "You tell those sons of bitches there that if they don't put this show on the air Monday," said the Governor, "I'll wreck this damn station of theirs here before sundown."

Truman's speech to the hundred thousand jammed in Cadillac Square and the millions of radio listeners zeroed right in on the Eightieth Congress: "If you stay at home, as you did in 1946, and keep these reactionaries in power, you will deserve every blow you get . . . The reactionary of today is a shrewd man. He is a man with a calculating machine where his heart ought to be . . .

"Labor has always had to fight for its gains . . . We are in a hard, tough fight against shrewd and rich opponents. They know they can't count on your vote. Their only hope is that you won't vote at all."

On September 17, the Truman Special pulled out of Washington for a practically continuous six-weeks tour. The whistlestop technique polished in the spring transcontinental trip was now perfected. At every stop the show went off like clockwork. As the high school band blared the "Missouri Waltz" Truman and the local Democratic contingent appeared on the ob-

Whistlestop, U.S.A. Battling against the odds, Truman put on a tremendous campaign, addressing major rallies and speaking informally to crowds gathered at railroad stations at all hours of day and night.

Bess and Margaret Truman accompanied him. "Our job was to render the situation normal," says Margaret. "Of course Mother looked after everybody—not only our own party but any member of the press corps who needed an aspirin or a button sewed on . . . We both endeavored to lend my father moral support—not that he needed it." His stamina amazed and exhausted aides and newspapermen.

Bess, Margaret, and Harry voted in Independence, while columnists, commentators, pollsters and editors unanimously predicted defeat.

servation platform. Bareheaded, smiling, right at home, introducing Democratic candidates as if he were introducing friends in the living room, he mixed kidding with seriousness. The Republicans, he said, were deaf to the voice of the people, although they could hear Wall Street all right. The Republican gifts to the country were the false boom of the 1920s and the Depression. "Republicans don't like to talk about 1932 and I don't blame them." And now the Republicans had produced that *"do-nothing, good-for-nothing Republican Eightieth Congress."* Depending on the area and audience, he hit specific failings of the do-nothing Congress: refusal to provide flexible price supports and other farm programs; refusal to restore price controls; passage over a veto of a rich man's tax-relief bill; a neo-isolationist failure to provide a home for the UN; the anti-labor Taft-Hartley law.

Congress thoroughly clobbered, Truman turned and brought Bess out on the platform. Until she put a stop to it one day in Ohio, he introduced her as "the Boss." Together, they were the image of a happily married pair of sixty-four-year-olds. Then, "Here's the one who bosses her!" and out stepped pretty, twenty-five-year-old Margaret with a bouquet of roses. The biggest hand of the day (or night) was accompanied by friendly whistles. When the train pulled out, with Truman leaning over the rail to shake all the hands he could reach, it was invariably accompanied by a running band of boys. Big boys and little boys, they all called out, "Goodby, Margaret!"

Again and again there were exchanges of dialogue. In Barstow, California, a lady called, "President Truman, you sound as if you had a cold!" To which the President responded, "That's because I ride around in the wind with my mouth open!"

Through September and October he made the incredible total of 356 speeches, morning, afternoon, evening, and midnight. To Jonathan Daniels, a distinguished former Roosevelt aide in the Truman entourage, the remarkable thing was "his ability to take his campaign easily and confidently. When the going was toughest and the rolling over the roadbeds roughest, he could make a 'give 'em hell, Harry' speech at one whistlestop and then go sound asleep before he was roused to make another, thirty minutes later . . . Strain seemed only to make him calmer and more firm."

It was as effective a campaign as a presidential candidate ever waged. Very few observers accurately assessed it. The Gallup, Crossley and Roper polls reported Dewey far in front, with Wallace and Thurmond registering small, important percentages.

Nobody questioned the figures. The polls had always been right, ever since Dr. Gallup had introduced his new technique of "scientific sampling" with spectacular success in the election of 1936.

The newsmen riding the Truman Special were entirely sympathetic and not one of them believed he could win. Richard Rovere, the astute correspondent of the *New Yorker,* describing the warmth of the crowds, wrote that the people appeared "ready to give Harry Truman anything in the world except the Presidency of the United States."

Abroad, Britain's foremost analyst of American politics, Alistair Cook, wrote an article for the *Manchester Guardian:* "Harry S Truman: A Study in Failure." Truman's future son-in-law, *New York Times* correspondent Clifton Daniel, Jr., dutifully reported the British expert's views to America. *The Economist* of London offered an ingenious explanation of the fact that Truman was drawing larger crowds than Dewey: "People who are convinced that they will have to vote for Dewey prefer not to be reminded." The *New York Times*'s top political correspondent, James Hagerty, carefully analyzed sentiment in the West, and awarded the entire region overwhelmingly to Dewey.

On October 11 *Newsweek* published a super-poll—the opinions of fifty leading newspaper experts from around the country. The fifty experts were unanimous. All fifty gave the election to Dewey. Not a single far-out gambler's vote for Truman.

His aides brought the magazine to Truman. He looked at it, grinned and said, "Forget it—they're always wrong." The aides went away thinking that if Truman had nothing else, he sure had guts.

Four days before the election the Gallup poll gave Dewey 49.5 percent of the popular vote, Truman 44.5 percent, with the rest to Wallace and Thurmond. The final Roper poll credited Dewey with 53 percent, Truman only 37½ percent. Speculation about Dewey's cabinet filled the columns of the bored pundits.

On October 30 Truman made a climactic speech to a tumultuous rally in St. Louis. Next day he was home in Independence to rest. On Election Eve, November 1, Senator Barkley, speaking from his own home in Paducah, Kentucky, introduced Truman, who delivered his final appeal to the voters— "to decide between the principles of the party for the people and the

Some newspapers even announced Dewey's victory next morning, despite the fact that Truman led the balloting from the start. That *Chicago Tribune* became a prize election souvenir. Another paper, the *Washington Post,* acknowledged its forecasting error by displaying sign to welcome Truman and Barkley back to the capital. As for the pollsters, a *Berkshire Evening Eagle* correspondent named L. S. Briggs neatly summed up their fiasco: O section, cross-section and sample,/O postcard and phone call and bell!/O Crossley, Roper and Gallup,/O George!/O Elmo!/O Hell!

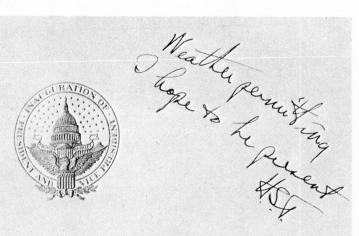

Weather permitting
I hope to be present
H.S.T.

The Inaugural Committee

requests the honor of the presence of

The President and Mrs. Truman

to attend and participate in the Inauguration of

Harry S. Truman

as President of the United States of America

and

Alben W. Barkley

as Vice President of the United States of America

on Thursday the twentieth of January

one thousand nine hundred and forty-nine

in the City of Washington

Please reply to
The Inaugural Committee
Tariff Building
Washington 25, D. C.

Melvin D. Hildreth

Chairman

R.S.V.P. On the formal invitation to the inauguration, Truman wrote in the upper right-hand corner, "Weather permitting, I hope to be present."

In top hats and striped trousers Truman and Barkley left Blair House at 11:30 A.M. for the cermony at the Capitol, accompanied by Bess, Margaret, and Barkley's daughter, Mrs. Max Truitt. The weather was beautiful, and fifteen hours later, at 3:30 A.M. Margaret wrote in her diary: "My feet hurt! But it has been a perfect Inauguration Day . . ."

party for the special interests." Then he went to bed and had a good sleep.

On Election Day he slipped away to Excelsior Springs, a nearby resort, to escape the reporters. He enjoyed a Turkish bath, retired to his room for a ham sandwich and a glass of milk, turned on the radio and listened to some of the first returns from the East.

They showed Truman leading. The radio commentators explained tolerantly that as soon as more precincts came in Dewey would take over. Many a dyed-in-the-wool Democrat shut off the radio and went gloomily to bed. Those who hung on began to feel a wild hope they hardly dared voice. In Excelsior Springs, Truman awoke at midnight. H. V. Kaltenborn, the dean of commentators, revealed that Truman was about 1,200,000 votes ahead, and certain to lose.

Truman turned over and went back to sleep. At 4 A.M. Jim Rowley, his chief Secret Service man, knocked on the door and suggested turning on the radio again. Kaltenborn now reported Truman two million votes ahead, with most of the country reporting—but Kaltenborn still could not see how he could win.

There was some justification for the fantastic radio blundering. Given the Electoral College system, a candidate can get a clear majority of the votes and lose—as Grover Cleveland did in 1888. Given minor-party candidates quite extraordinary results are possible. With Strom Thurmond taking the 38 electoral votes of four southern states, Truman had to carry more northern and western states than he otherwise would have needed. The Wallace vote, though smaller than expected, was enough to put at least three states, New York, Michigan and Maryland, with 74 electoral votes, in the Republican column. But Truman carried Wisconsin, Minnesota, Ohio and Illinois despite Wallace, and in fact made an excellent showing throughout the Midwest and West. He wound up with 304 electoral votes to Dewey's 189.

Less easy to excuse is the failure of the polls correctly to assess the Truman margin in popular votes. Outside the Electoral College the election was not really close. Dewey lost by well over two million. His percentage was actually down slightly from 1944—45.1 from 45.8, instead of up to 49.5 as Gallup had predicted. Dewey himself always believed that he lost through Republican stay-at-homes, though the figures themselves do not necessarily suggest this.

The Wallace danger certainly faded in the closing days of the campaign, when many liberals began to have second thoughts. And the Dixiecrat revolt was not as menacing as it might appear at first glance, because the 38 electoral votes, though taken from the Democratic column, did not go into the Republican column, and so represented a net loss of only 19½.

But the failure of the pundits and pollsters remains a mystery, with a suspicion that part of the monumental miscalculation derived from the notion that an ordinary-looking man from Missouri, wearing steel-rimmed glasses and with no resonance in his voice, could not win a presidential election. They forgot that Lincoln was a homely Midwesterner with a poor speaking voice.

A month after the election Truman attended the Army-Navy game in Philadelphia. A Navy team that had lost every game on its schedule was up against an Army super-team that had not lost a game in years. At half-time, Navy cheerleaders paraded the field with a sign:

GALLUP PICKS ARMY

Navy's courageous team went on to tie Army for the second biggest upset of the year.

A PORTFOLIO

The southpaw President kept up a
White House tradition, and with Con-
nie Mack, manager of the Philadelphia Athletics, center, and Clark
Griffith, president of the Washington
Senators, looking on, threw out the
first pitch of the Senators' opening
game in 1949.

Forthright speechmaker. The President, always the plain Midwestern from Missouri, was highly regarded as a public speaker for his clear, man-to-man expression of ideas. Whether in black tie or at a county fair, Truman knew how to put his thoughts across to his audience.

The President as official host. There was rarely a letup in the social calendar for Truman, who was continually greeting heads of state and visiting dignitaries at Blair House. Here, three of the most famous guests: Winston Churchill, Princess (later Queen) Elizabeth, and General Eisenhower.

Shirtsleeve press conference in Key West, Florida, favorite retreat of the President.

Famous Truman grin was depicted by more than forty of the nation's top cartoonists and comic strip artists who came to the White House for the beginning of a nation-wide tour to promote savings bonds.

The President and "Mister Sam." A good part of Truman's political success since his senatorial days was due to the close friendship between him and Speaker of the House Sam Rayburn of Texas, shown here in Key West. The two often met in the late afternoon to exchange information and "strike a blow for liberty" with a peg of bourbon.

Always a family man, the President was a faithful correspondent with his mother and sister in Independence, and liked to spend as much time with Bess and Margaret as possible. Whenever he could arrange to pass through St. Louis he would visit his sister Mary, shown greeting him at the airport, and his mother, here at the age of ninety-two.

1949–1952

THE COLD WAR TURNS HOT

Inauguration DAY, January 20, 1949, started off with a sentimental breakfast get-together of ninety-eight veterans of Battery D, the old "Truman Battery." As his buddies crowded around to shake hands they addressed their former CO as "Mr. President," but he put a stop to it. "We'll have none of that here," he said. "You'll call me Captain Harry, just like you did in the Argonne thirty years ago."

The 129th's old regimental chaplain now Monsignor L. Curtis Tiernan, and chief of chaplains for the European Theatre in World War II, said grace, and the gang settled down to refighting the Battle of Who Run. Afterward they all marched down Pennsylvania Avenue as a special honor guard in the inaugural parade.

As he took the oath from Chief Justice Vinson, Harry Truman's one regret was that his mother could not have lived to be present. Martha Young Truman had died eighteen months earlier at the age of ninety-four.

The inaugural address contained a surprise package for press and public. Ever since the success of the Marshall Plan and Truman Doctrine, Truman and Acheson had been considering another problem—helping the new countries which were rapidly emerging from the old colonial empires. Most of these countries were "underdeveloped" or "undeveloped." Lacking both industry and modern agricultural methods, they were not susceptible to the sort of economic-transfusion approach that had been so effective in Western Europe. Yet it seemed highly expedient to find a way to help them, not merely to keep them from turning to Communism, but to keep them from becoming seas of dangerous discontent.

Now, as "Point Four" of a four-point program, Truman put forward an entirely new idea in American foreign policy. Along with the Marshall Plan, Truman Doctrine and support of UN, he asserted that the U.S. "must embark on a bold new program for making the benefits of our scientific advances and industrial progress available for the improvement and growth of underdeveloped areas." The economies of the emerging countries had to be built from the ground up, something that could only be accomplished over a long period, with hard work by the people and well-planned assistance, both technical and financial, from the U.S.

Point Four, widely discussed in the press, aroused surprisingly little opposition and became almost at once an accepted part of America's responsibility in the world. Under varying names, it has continued to operate through every administration since.

The spring of 1949 saw two parallel dramas reach a climax in Europe— NATO and the Berlin Airlift. The four-power division of Germany had crystallized into a West-vs.-East split in which two divergent policies were pursued by the rival occupying powers. The U.S.-dominated Western occupation zones benefited from a friendly, democratic and liberal regime which set to work to rebuild the German economy. The Soviet Zone, on the other hand, was unceremoniously despoiled of everything usable for shipment to Russia. Russia's attitude was understandable, but self-defeating, and seriously exacerbated inter-Allied relations. It lay at the bottom of a dispute over German currency which boiled up in the Allied Control Council in 1948. Stalin attempted to pressure the Western Allies by refusing to permit passage of truck convoys across the Soviet Zone of Germany to the Western Zone of Berlin. Truman's response was interesting. Instead of making a demand backed by the threat of war, he used American air power in a non-violent way to sidestep the Russian blockade. Supplies formerly trucked to West Berlin were flown in. The technical success of the operation was impressive, and in the spring of 1949 Stalin gave in and reopened the truck highway.

The Berlin crisis gave a prod to the development of a military alliance between Western Europe and the United States. The original germ was a treaty Britain and France signed at Dunkirk immediately after the war, aimed at Germany. By early 1948 Truman and Marshall were encouraging the British and French to expand their alliance to include other West European states, and pressing for a frank re-orientation against Russia. Prolonged negotiations, complicated principally by the Europeans' distrust of West Germany, which the Americans wanted to bring into the alliance, were carried to a successful conclusion by Acheson, the new Secretary of State. The formal alliance, signed in Washington in April 1949, included twelve nations: France, Britain, the Benelux countries, Canada, Norway, Denmark, Iceland, Portugal, Italy and the United States. West Germany, Greece, and Turkey were added later. The problem of constitutional limitations on the President's war-making powers was solved by a Canadian compromise proposal by which all parties to the treaty agreed to come to the aid of a victim of aggression in accordance with their various constitutional processes.

The North Atlantic Treaty Organization did not win universal approval at home. Critics on the right and on the left joined in attacking the commitment as a dangerous provocation to Russia. Senator Taft declared his opposition based on the conclusion that "the pact carries with it an obligation to assist in arming, at our expense, the nations of Western Europe, because with that obligation I believe it will promote war in the world rather than peace, and because I think that with the arms plan it is wholly contrary to the spirit of the obligations we assumed in the United Nations Charter. If Russia sees itself ringed about gradually by so-called defensive arms, from Norway and Denmark to Turkey and Greece, it may . . . decide that the arming . . . looks to an attack upon Russia."

Henry Wallace came close to echoing these sentiments: "Stripped of legal verbiage; the North Atlantic military pact gives the United States Army military bases up to the very borders of the Soviet Union . . . Does anyone imagine that, as they stare across their borders at our jet bombers and our cannon, calm visions of peace will be born in their minds? . . . Supposing the Soviets had military bases on the Mexican border? The Canadian border? On Cuba?"

Truman did not waver. As NATO spelled out America's commitment to European defense, the American military establishment itself was undergoing a significant change. Truman had always been on the affirmative side of the long-standing controversy over unification of the armed forces. By May of 1946 he had managed to get the main areas of disagreement between Navy and Army clearly identified, and after a considerable struggle these were resolved in the National Security Act of 1947, which set up a three-branched service with the added element of a Central Intelligence Agency. In the spring of 1949 the act was amended to provide an Undersecretary and a Chairman of the Joint Chiefs of Staff, who formed a powerful top policy committee.

The now intense Cold War with Russia, reflected in these new aspects of American government and policy, found a more bitter and less constructive expression in a growing national hysteria over spies. That the Soviet Union carried out extensive espionage operations in the U.S. was first revealed publicly with the defection of a Russian embassy attaché in Canada late in 1945. The most alarming side of his disclosures was the news that the Soviets had obtained an undetermined amount of information on the atomic bomb. In 1950 the belated arrest by the British of their German-born nuclear physicist Klaus Fuchs supplied dismaying corroboration of the success of Soviet atomic espionage. Long before that some far less significant, non-atomic espionage revelations made tremendous impact on the public consciousness because of their peculiarly sensational character. A woman named Elizabeth Bentley, who had acted as a courier for a Soviet ring in Washington, made a confession to the FBI in New Haven in 1945 which the FBI found so hard to believe that it was not repeated in public till the Turnip Session of Congress in 1948. A Treasury Department official, Harry Dexter White, implicated by Miss Bentley, denied the charges before the House Un-American Activities Committee and then died of a heart attack.

An even more sensational case developed when a senior editor of *Time* magazine named Whittaker Chambers disclosed that he too had been a Soviet courier in Washington in the 1930s, and implicated a distinguished former State Department official named Alger Hiss, who in 1948 held the eminent post of president of the Carnegie Endowment for World Peace. Hiss truculently denied Chambers' charges, and out of his denials grew a perjury trial which resulted in a hung jury. Early in 1950 a second trial resulted in a conviction and a stiff five-year prison sentence. The fact that the Hiss case took the legal form of a perjury trial tended to obscure the nature of the alleged espionage. The information transmitted, dating to 1937–38, consisted of State Department messages and memoranda, mostly pertaining to Nazi Germany and Japan. The statute of limitations had run out on charges based directly on the alleged acts. But Hiss's decision to fight, and the dramatic, long-drawn-out duel with Chambers that followed, turned Hiss into the major symbol of treason inside the government, of which an exaggerated fear swept the country. Even in the '48 campaign Dewey was able to make effective use of the spy issue. Had Alger Hiss

The Berlin Airlift. The split between Western Allies and Soviet Russia over administration of defeated Germany was brought to a head by a Russian blockade of the Western Zone of Berlin in 1948. Truman's response avoided war without backing down: West Berlin was effectively supplied by a gigantic American air operation. This intensity light was installed to guide planes in despite fog and darkness.

Birth of NATO. Truman and Eisenhower conferred before Eisenhower's departure for Europe in early 1950 to head the new treaty organization. They review an honor guard at National Airport, Washington.

The rise of McCarthyism. Revelations of Communist spy rings operating inside the government led to a wave of hysteria on which conservative politicians, especially Senator McCarthy of Wisconsin, capitalized.

ABOVE, Senator McCarthy (third from right, hand on mouth) conducts a publicity-charged hearing of his Senate subcommittee on internal security. Truman took steps to protect security, but denounced McCarthy: "It is one of the tragedies of our time that the security program of the United States has been wickedly used by demagogues and sensational newspapers in an attempt to frighten and mislead the American people."

RIGHT, Elizabeth Bentley, another confessed spy, whose testimony implicated several government officials.

Confessed Soviet spy Whittaker Chambers (upper left, standing with dark tie, white shirt) dramatically confronts former State Department official Alger Hiss (standing, right). Hiss's denial that he transmitted confidential State Department documents to Russia led to two perjury trials and a five-year prison term.

Scandal. As if President Truman did not have enough problems with his enemies, his friends caused him some too. General Harry Vaughan, his old AEF buddy, got in trouble with Congress by doing favors that the Congress said bordered on corruption.

been convicted two years earlier it is doubtful that Truman could have been re-elected.

During the month after Hiss's sentencing Senator Joseph R. McCarthy of Wisconsin, an ex-Marine captain and judge, demonstrated how the national phobia could be exploited with a sensational speech in the unlikely precincts of the Republican Women's Club of Wheeling, West Virginia. Senator McCarthy repeated the already familiar Republican charge that the State Department, headed by Dean Acheson, an old friend and former colleague of Alger Hiss, was honeycombed with Communists. What made Senator McCarthy's use of the charge amazingly effective was his pseudo-documentation in the form of an alleged list of two hundred and five names of State Department employees who were "card-carrying members or certainly loyal to the Communist Party." A Senate committee appointed to investigate the charge found that McCarthy's information was a "colored and distorted version of material developed by investigators of the House Appropriations Committee in 1947 during the Eightieth Congress," and totally misleading. But McCarthy's technique was spectacularly successful throughout the country, where overnight he acquired a national following. Loyalty investigations, self-appointed vigilante groups and other witch hunters, professional and amateur, sprang up from New York to California.

Truman did not lose his head merely because others were losing theirs. He refused to take the lurid charges against the State Department seriously, and characterized the Eightieth Congress's spy hearings as "a red herring" used by the Republicans to avoid coming to grips with the nation's problems. He had already established a federal Commission on Employee Loyalty which was carrying out a painstaking security check on a massive scale, but his attitude toward McCarthy and the House Un-American Activities Committee brought him violent abuse from the extreme Right.

Behind the loyalty-security hysteria lay the frustrations of the Cold War— the intractability of the Russians, the success of the Chinese Communists and the sinister Pandora's box of nuclear weapons. However much aid they got from their spies, the Russians produced their first atomic explosion in 1949, more than ten years ahead of General Groves' prediction. (A Pentagon estimate the year before forecast the Soviet bomb for 1952, and intercontinental missiles by 1977.) World Communism, which was taken to be a single massive fabric despite a break between Tito of Yugoslavia and Moscow, seemed to be on the offensive. Once confined to Russia's 1939

Assassination attempt was made by two fanatical Puerto Rican nationalists who tried to shoot their way into Blair House November 1, 1950, but were gunned down by White House guards. Truman left at once by car, followed by an open automobile of Secret Service men.

boundaries, it had spread over Eastern Europe, penetrated Central Europe with the coup in Czechoslovakia, and won control of all China, whence it threatened to overflow the rest of Asia.

It was against this background that on June 24, 1950, Truman received an urgent telephone call from Secretary of State Acheson in the middle of a weekend at home in Independence. It was Saturday evening, and the Trumans were sitting in the library of the North Delaware Street house. Acheson was calling from his own home in Maryland. "Mr. President," he said, "I have very serious news. The North Koreans have invaded South Korea."

Acheson had few details. He recommended asking for a meeting of the UN Security Council to condemn the aggression.

On Sunday morning Acheson telephoned again. The Security Council was meeting in emergency session. But while it would probably call for a cease-fire, there was little likelihood of the North Koreans paying any attention. It was now evident that the invasion was on a major scale, and a decision had to be made at once on the degree of help or encouragement the U.S. would give South Korea. Truman directed Acheson to get together with the Service Secretaries and Chiefs of Staff and start working on recommendations to be ready for him on his arrival. In less than an hour his plane was taking off from Kansas City Municipal Airport.

After a hasty dinner at Blair House (the White House had been undergoing repairs for some time) the assembled military and government officials listened to Acheson's report and recommendations. The Security Council had condemned the aggression, and called on UN members to help halt it, but a report on the military situation from the U.S. ambassador to South Korea was ominous. U.S. aid was imperatively needed. It was not clear whether air and naval support would suffice. Truman's decision was that the aggression must be stopped at whatever cost. There was no dissent. For the time being General MacArthur, commander-in-chief in the Far East, was ordered to give the South Korean army ammunition and supplies, while the U. S. Seventh Fleet, at the moment en route from Japan to the Philippines, was ordered to occupy the Formosa Strait, in order to intercept a possible Chinese Communist attack on Formosa.

On Monday Truman received an appeal for help from Syngman Rhee, the strong-minded anti-Communist president of the Republic of Korea. Later the same day a cable came from MacArthur who had made a firsthand inspection at the front: . . . SOUTH KOREAN UNITS UNABLE TO RESIST DETERMINED NORTHERN OFFENSIVE. CONTRIBUTORY FACTOR EXCLUSIVE ENEMY POSSESSION OF TANKS AND FIGHTER PLANES. SOUTH KOREAN CASUALTIES AS AN INDEX TO FIGHTING HAVE NOT SHOWN ADEQUATE RESISTANCE CAPABILITIES OR THE WILL TO FIGHT AND OUR ESTIMATE IS THAT A COMPLETE COLLAPSE IS IMMINENT.

Truman telephoned MacArthur on the scrambler phone and directed him to give immediate air and naval assistance to the South Koreans. At the same time he approved recommendations for strengthening American forces in the Philippines and for giving increased aid to the French in Indochina.

In these various responses can be seen the conviction, shared by Truman, Acheson and all other policymakers, that the North Korean attack was a chess move by world Communism, and that further moves in other areas were to be anticipated as part of the pattern of Communist global offensive. A hint that such might not be the case lay in the UN Security Council action, made possible only by the absence of the Soviet Ambassador, who had walked out of the Council to protest the continued seating of Chiang Kai-shek's Ambassador as the representative of China.

But if he exaggerated the Kremlin's role in launching the North Korean aggression, Truman did not let the assumption carry him away. If it had to be war, he was sure that a small war was better than a big one, and determined to keep it as small as possible. Therefore, while acceding to a request from MacArthur to commit an American regimental combat team and build up to two divisions, he turned down an offer from Chiang Kai-shek of 33,000 Nationalist Chinese troops and scrubbed an Air Force plan to fly reconnaissance missions over Soviet Far East bases. In Truman's view, it was important not to give the Russians a "pretext" for intervention in Korea. Russian terminology for such flights would certainly have been "provocation."

MacArthur's early estimate of the course of the fighting was accurate. The South Korean army was quickly overpowered by its North Korean rival. Seoul, the South Korean capital, fell, and the disorganized fragments of the defending army retreated south toward Pusan, at the base of the peninsula. In this situation MacArthur was forced to commit piecemeal American occupation troops from Japan. But additional units from Hawaii and the continental U.S. permitted a strong perimeter defense to be established by the Eighth Army, under Lieutenant General Walton H. Walker, around Pusan.

As the end of summer approached, the heavy fighting ground into stale-

War breaks out in Korea. Without
warning, on June 24, 1950, Commu-
nist North Korean Premier Kim Il-
Sung, ABOVE, launched an invasion of
South Korea, whose government was
headed by staunch anti-Communist
President Syngman Rhee, BELOW.
Four days later Seoul, the South
Korean capital, had fallen and the
South Korean army was fleeing south-
ward.

mate. MacArthur then launched a spectacular counterblow which he had envisioned almost from the beginning—an amphibious assault on Inchon, the port of Seoul, far behind the North Korean army's fighting front. The move was a daring gamble, because owing to the strong tides it had to be made on one precise day, September 15, when the enemy might be expected to be alerted. But the landing, spearheaded by the 1st Marine Division, was a success, and soon the whole North Korean army was streaming north from Pusan, hotly pursued by the Eighth Army and harried by the Air Force. This sensational reversal of the tide of battle seemed to be the fruit of MacArthur's genius. Actually, it was owing more to the swift American build-up, which had created a numerical superiority of two-to-one and a fire-power superiority of six-to-one at Pusan. The North Korean commander had had little to spare for defense of Inchon and Seoul. Had the X Corps, which MacArthur employed at Inchon, been committed instead at Pusan, it is likely that the result would have been the same, with less risk.

A far graver hazard lay immediately ahead. With the broken enemy fleeing homeward, the question arose on the victors' side of where to stop. The 38th parallel of latitude, hastily selected in 1945 by the U.S. and accepted by Russia, was an arbitrary boundary, separating two synthetic states, North and South Korea. Since the Communist North had started the war with the aim of unifying the country under Communism, it seemed to Syngman Rhee only reasonable to take advantage of the opportunity to unify the country under his own regime. The China bloc in the U.S. gave them support. Not to cross the 38th parallel, they warned, would be appeasement. Most of the public felt the same way. Truman, who had been careful to limit the original military commitment to action south of the parallel, now gave in to the public clamor for total victory.

In the UN, Acheson was reversing his field and rounding up support for unification of Korea by force. Ernest Bevin, Britain's Labour Foreign Secretary, enthusiastically joined in. A British resolution was voted by the General Assembly 47 to 5, with only seven abstentions—five Arab countries, Yugoslavia and India.

The euphoria of victory blinded nearly everyone, and above all MacArthur, who was reveling in his strategic masterpiece. In mid-October Truman flew to meet MacArthur at Wake Island. His main concern was to impress on MacArthur what Washington called the global picture, which meant the importance of not letting the Korean war get too big, lest with American power tied up, Russia should "start something" in Europe.

There was, however, a second reason for the meeting. Douglas MacArthur occupied a unique position, sometimes characterized as "an American pro-consulship." From his Tokyo headquarters he reigned as military lord of the Far East. He had not visited the U.S. in fourteen years, since well before Pearl Harbor. Despite this, or because of it, his military successes and his flair for self-dramatization had made him a tremendous popular hero, especially on the Right. He often made policy pronouncements on his own initiative, and a few weeks earlier had sent a message to the Veterans of Foreign Wars on the military value of Formosa to the U.S. which did not read particularly well abroad. Truman wanted to give the egocentric general a gentle reminder about who was the commander-in-chief under the Constitution.

As images, the two men presented a striking contrast—MacArthur tall, handsome, casually uniformed, with sunglasses setting off his personally designed cap; Truman neat and unobtrusive in a double-breasted business suit.

They began with a private meeting which proved surprisingly cordial.

MacArthur apologized for the embarrassment caused by his message to the VFW and expressed his intention of staying out of politics. Most of the talk was about the future, after the war had been won. MacArthur figured that most of the Eighth Army could be withdrawn by Christmas, the rest after elections in January. A unified, democratic Korea, armed with "about ten divisions with our equipment . . . a small but competent air force and . . . navy" would "not only secure Korea but . . . be a tremendous deterrent to the Chinese Communists moving south . . . a threat that cannot be laughed off."

Truman put the question: "What are the chances for Chinese or Soviet intervention?"

MacArthur's answer was categorical: "Very little . . . We are no longer fearful of their intervention . . . The Chinese have three hundred thousand men in Manchuria. Of these probably not more than one hundred to one hundred twenty-five thousand are distributed along the Yalu River. Only fifty to sixty thousand could be gotten across . . . They have no air force. Now that we have bases for our Air Force in Korea, if the Chinese tried to get down to Pyongyang (the North Korean capital) there would be the greatest slaughter."

Truman hurried back to Washington from Independence and made the momentuous decision to give military support to the South Koreans. Within days, American and South Korean troops were fighting side by side.

Truman vs. MacArthur. After General MacArthur's successful counterattack against the North Koreans, the general was estimating that the fighting could be ended by Christmas of 1950. Truman, ABOVE, seen off at Washington's National Airport by Secretary of State Acheson, flew to Wake Island to confer with MacArthur in October. Confident of complete victory, MacArthur discounted possible intervention by the new Chinese Communist government.

But Chinese troops were already pouring across the Yalu River every night, and MacArthur's new offensive north of the 38th parallel ran into a severe defeat. The general's desire to expand the war with air and naval attacks on China, and his insubordination in pressing his views, led to his dismissal by Truman early in 1951.

MacArthur also assessed the potential of Russian intervention. The Russians, he said, had a strong air force in Siberia but no ground forces near the narrow Soviet-North Korean border. "It would take six weeks to get a division across, and six weeks brings the winter. The only other combination would be Russian air support of Chinese ground troops . . . the coordination . . . would be so flimsy that I believe Russian air would bomb the Chinese as often as they would bomb us . . ."

MacArthur in any case did not believe South Korean troops would suffice to pacify North Korea.

The UN advance continued. On October 19 Pyongyang, the North Korean capital, was occupied. A week later, on October 26, the X Corps identified Chinese prisoners of war, taken in some very sharp combat. Further, the prisoners said they had crossed the Yalu on October 16.

The news was received with surprising calmness by MacArthur, the Joint Chiefs and Truman. They all assumed that the Chinese entry was on a very limited scale—a handful of volunteers, or semi-volunteers. The truth was, MacArthur's intelligence had failed badly. At the moment MacArthur was reassuring Truman on Wake Island, four Chinese armies of 120,000 men were already in North Korea, and by the end of October 180,000 more had crossed entirely undetected. The Chinese moved solely at night, hiding men and trucks in daytime.

On November 4, MacArthur reaffirmed the view that the Chinese intervention, though certainly real, was probably on a limited basis and recommended "against hasty conclusions." But two days later he ordered a major air strike against the Yalu bridges. This threatened to violate a commitment the British had extracted from Acheson not to carry the fighting into Manchuria. A message to MacArthur ordered postponement of the mission and asked for an explanation of the sudden turnaround. In reply, on November 6, just two days after his "hasty conclusions" message, MacArthur delivered the astounding news that "Men and material in large force are pouring across all bridges over the Yalu . . . This movement . . . threatens the ultimate destruction of the forces under my command . . . Your instructions may well result in a calamity of major proportions . . ."

MacArthur urged that the matter be taken up with the President, as in fact it already had been. But in view of the extreme urgency of the general's new communication, Truman decided to give permission to bomb the bridges, specifying only that Manchurian soil should not be hit.

Next day, November 7, MacArthur was more cautious. He referred again to his earlier estimate that the Chinese intervention was limited, even though it might reach "a point rendering our resumption of advance impossible and even forcing a movement in retrograde." Later the same day he reported a new and ominous development: "Hostile planes are operating from bases west of the Yalu River . . . in increasing numbers." Now he wanted permission for his air force to pursue enemy planes over Chinese soil.

He still underestimated the danger, and on the basis of his reports so did Truman and the Joint Chiefs. At the National Security Council meeting on November 9, Acheson voiced highly unrealistic suggestions about a demilitarized zone on both sides of the Yalu, and on November 24 MacArthur actually launched a new offensive, designed to get the fighting over by Christmas.

The new offensive ran head-on into the full power which the Chinese had silently deployed south of the Yalu—some half a million men. Furthermore, the quality of the Chinese troops was first class. They were well-armed, warmly uniformed, adequately supplied, well-led and with high morale. They attacked with ferocity and fought tenaciously. They did not remind anybody of Chiang Kai-shek's troops.

Nevertheless, as the Allies pulled back, badly mauled, MacArthur's manpower shortage caused him to request a reconsideration of Chiang's offer of 33,000 troops from Formosa. Truman promised to review the question. Actually sentiment in the United Nations forbade the move. The Europeans, led by the British, were apprehensive about any enlargement of the conflict and particularly fearful that their powerful American ally might be tempted to use the atomic bomb.

Their fears were not entirely groundless. At the first crisis of the war, when the Eighth Army stood beleaguered in the Pusan perimeter, General Thomas S. Power's Strategic Air Command had been ordered to stand by. Now these orders were repeated. At a press conference Truman stated that the U.S. would "take whatever steps are necessary to meet the military situation." Pressed specifically on the atomic bomb, he replied, "That includes every weapon we have." Given the form of presidential press conferences, it was difficult to avoid some such statement, since to assert that the bomb would not be used, or would be used only in certain specific circumstances, would be to give valuable information to the enemy. But one hundred Labour MP's promptly signed a petition, and Clement Attlee flew over to remonstrate with tact and skill. In a conference with Truman and Acheson, he brought up the idea of a cease-fire. Acheson, outlining the American policy position, emphasized that the main enemy was not Chiang but Soviet Russia, which in U.S. opinion had instigated the war in the first place. Attlee was less sure than Truman and Acheson that the Chinese Communists were "Russian satellites," and went so far as to express his conviction that Communist China should be admitted to the UN and given Formosa.

In a second meeting, aboard the presidential yacht, Truman told Attlee that the U.S. had to stand firm in Korea because "we cannot desert our friends when the going gets rough." Attlee assured Truman that "we stand with you." Truman concluded: "Loyalty to principles and friends, and also to treaty commitments, is a British attitude." Diplomatic finesse was also a British attitude, and Attlee must certainly be given credit for placing a restraining hand on Truman at a moment when dangerous pressure was being put on him in the other direction, toward all-out war with China and/or Russia. A resolution was introduced by Republicans in Congress demanding to be informed about "secret commitments" to Attlee. The men behind it Truman accurately described as seeing "nothing wrong in plunging headlong into an Asian war but would raise no finger for the defense of Europe; [they] thought a British Prime Minister was never to be trusted but Chiang Kai-shek could do no wrong."

Military defeat was creating an extraordinary degree of frustration and bitterness in the U.S., especially among conservatives. MacArthur's demands for Chiang Kai-shek's troops and for permission to pursue enemy planes into Manchuria were now being raised to include air and naval action against Manchuria and China proper. Republicans in Congress were clamoring for the dismissal of Dean Acheson, not on the grounds that Acheson had made mistakes but on the grounds that he was some sort of traitor.

At this moment an interesting shift in the military command took place with little public notice. General Walker, commanding the Eighth Army, was killed in a jeep accident, and General Matthew B. Ridgway, replacing him, was given command of the X Corps as well as the Eighth Army. By this slight alteration MacArthur was deprived of a field-command function, though his role as theatre commander was untouched.

The Chinese drove steadily south along both sides of the central mountain ridge, capturing Pyongyang and Seoul. The UN Army now numbered more than 350,000 men, half American, most of the rest South Korean, but with at least token representation from Britain, France, Turkey, Greece, Australia and other U.S. allies. Lengthening supply lines presently brought the Chinese offensive to a halt, and Ridgway soon mounted a counteroffensive. He attempted nothing grandiose, like the Inchon operation, but contented himself with pressing for limited objectives and doing maximum damage with his air power. Chinese casualties, including prisoners, rose. By March the UN forces had again retaken Seoul and reached the 38th parallel. The moment had arrived, in the eyes of the British and European allies, to seek an armistice.

Now came the climax of the Truman-MacArthur drama. Preliminary to seeking a cease-fire, a message was sent to MacArthur explaining that a UN offer of armistice would soon be made, and asking "what authority you should have to permit sufficient freedom of action for next few weeks to provide security for United Nations forces and maintain contact with enemy." MacArthur replied that his present directive was adequate, that no further restrictions should be placed on him, and that with the existing limitations and the size of his forces it was not practicable to attempt to clear North Korea of the enemy.

Marshall (now Secretary of Defense), Acheson, and the Joint Chiefs went to work on a presidential announcement, which the State Department undertook to clear with major allied governments. The draft was short and simple, made no boasts and uttered no threats, but pointed out that with the opposing forces aligned roughly on the 38th parallel a basis existed for ending the fighting. The draft was never published. Before negotiations with the allies could be concluded MacArthur undercut the whole diplomatic offensive by issuing his own offer to negotiate with the enemy commander "in the field"—accompanying the offer with a menacing reference to an air and naval attack on China, an attack which he asserted "would doom Red China to the risk of imminent military collapse." It was, as Truman observed, "a most extraordinary statement for a military commander to issue on his own responsibility." More than that, it was an egregious blunder. The notion that Mao and Chou could be shaken by the threat of air raids and naval bombardments was a bad miscalculation. As this became apparent in the emphatic silence from Peking, MacArthur's days as proconsul were numbered. Truman's first move was to announce that the decision on where to halt the current UN advance would be made on grounds of "tactical security"—meaning Ridgway, not MacArthur. For the moment that was as

Reactions of shock and anger erupted in Washington and across the nation when the announcement of MacArthur's dismissal was made public. And when the general came back home he was given a super-hero's welcome from San Francisco, ABOVE, to New York. MacArthur addressed Congress with persuasive eloquence, but his declaration that "There is no substitute for victory" did not convince the lawmakers or the public.

Secretary of Defense Marshall flew to Tokyo to confer on the Korean military situation with MacArthur's successor, General Matthew B. Ridgway.

The war dragged on, in spite of predictions and hopes to the contrary, and would not be resolved throughout the Truman administration.

far as he went, but the ultimate clash was now inevitable and could not long be postponed. MacArthur supplied the pretext himself by still another incredible piece of effrontery. In reply to a letter from Joe Martin, Republican leader of the House, about using Chiang's troops, he not only openly took issue with the government's policy but went on to a lofty declaration that "here we fight Europe's war with arms while the diplomats there still fight it with words; that if we lose this war to Communism in Asia the fall of Europe is inevitable . . . There is no substitute for victory."

It is probable that MacArthur overestimated the importance of his wide popular support in the U.S. and the influence of his friends in Congress and the press. It is almost certain that he underestimated Harry Truman.

The order relieving MacArthur of his command was sent to Secretary of the Army Frank Pace, then in Korea, to be handed personally to the general. Before this could be done a press leak threatened. Truman called a quick 1 A.M. press conference and had news releases distributed. As a result, MacArthur had to be rather ungraciously notified by radio.

The storm that broke in Congress and the press was by far the biggest of Truman's entire administration. Senator William E. Jenner declared the country to be "in the hands of a secret inner coterie which is directed by agents of the Soviet Union," and called for impeachment of Truman, a question that Joe Martin said was under discussion among top Republican leaders. Senator Richard Nixon contented himself with calling for a motion of censure.

Significantly, no responsible individual or group, including the military, questioned Truman's right to fire MacArthur. Significantly too, press comment abroad was favorable. *Le Monde* of Paris took up an American newspaper's angry gibe at "a haberdasher firing a five-star general." That, said *Le Monde*, was precisely what democracy was all about—that five-star generals should be subject to the orders of haberdashers.

What *Le Monde* might have added was that this was no ordinary haberdasher. Truman knew the powers of the presidency, and knew its history—he thought of Lincoln's problem with McClellan—but more than that, he had the nerve. Although he had experienced no difficulty in getting concurrence from Marshall, Bradley, and the Joint Chiefs—most of MacArthur's military compeers were heartily sick of his grandiloquence—he would have gone ahead without it.

The popular explosion over MacArthur's dismissal concealed the fact that a chance to end the war had been missed. MacArthur was brought home to a record-breaking hero's welcome, New York lining its streets and skyscrapers with seven and a half million people, and loosing twice as much ticker tape as it had showered on Lindbergh. But behind the emotion lay little public conviction about Korea. In Congress MacArthur made an eloquent address, adding a new phrase to the nation's vocabulary with his sentimental closing: "Old soldiers never die, they just fade away." But in the Senate hearing room, he made far less impression. His assertion that Korea was the last chance for the U.S. to defeat the dark powers of Communism brought the query, "Alone?" To which MacArthur's response of, "Alone, if necessary," left him practically without legislative support. Popular emotion damned Truman; rational discussion damned MacArthur.

In Korea the Chinese mounted a spring offensive, to which Ridgway replied with a counteroffensive. The two bloody actions confirmed the stalemate, and a fresh decision was taken not to attempt an invasion of North Korea. As Ridgway pointed out, even an advance to the Yalu would not end the war, but merely quadruple the length of the front.

A "Little Armistice," achieved in November 1951, turned the war into one of patrol actions, interrupted by a costly limited offensive the following fall, carried out mostly by South Korean troops. The halt to the fighting was not finally formalized until July of 1953. Stalin's death in March 1953 may have been a factor in a Soviet peace initiative in the UN.

By that time MacArthur had retired to a suite in the Waldorf Towers in New York and Truman was back home in Independence.

MR. HARRY TRUMAN

THE KOREAN war dominated Truman's second administration. Its costs put an end to the balanced budgets in which he had taken pride and had a negative effect on further social-welfare legislation. The Housing Act of 1949, an important achievement, was virtually the last of the Fair Deal. Medicare and other measures had to await a more favorable climate. The liberal Brannan Plan reforming farm subsidies was beaten by the opposition of the rich farmers' organizations.

Reactionary legislation tended to dominate the congressional scene. The Internal Security Act, passed in the heat of the war, drew a thoughtfully worded Truman veto, over which it was repassed at once. Truman felt that the law violated an important American axiom—"that we punish men for the crimes they commit but never for the opinions they have." The McCarran-Walter Immigration Act of 1952 froze the discriminatory quotas against southern and eastern Europeans and Asians. Truman pointed out in his veto message that there were 138,000 anti-Communist Poles in exile, but the new law would admit only 6,500 of them a year; that 23,000 anti-Soviet refugees from the Baltic countries were confronted with a quota of 700, and 30,000 refugee Romanians with one of 289. In addition, the Attorney General was empowered to deport any alien who had engaged in activities "prejudicial to the public interest" or "subversive to the national security." Truman called the act "worse than the infamous Alien Act of 1798," but Congress again overrode his veto.

The generally regressive tone even infected the Supreme Court, which disappointed Truman by refusing to uphold his seizure of the steel companies to halt a strike in 1952.

At the same time two other developments were casting shadows. One was the continuing success of Senator McCarthy, whose stature was assuming menacing proportions. The other was the "scandals." The *New York Herald Tribune* uncovered the influence of certain lobbyists who came to be known as the "five percenters" because of the fee they exacted for their influence on behalf of clients in the War Assets Administration and elsewhere. The central figure in the investigation that followed was jovial Harry Vaughan, Truman's oldest, closest buddy from the Argonne, now a brigadier general and the President's military aide. Harry Vaughan was not a crook, but he had used poor judgment in doing favors for friends, and the press had a field day. Subsequent scandals involving the Bureau of Internal Revenue (now the Internal Revenue Service) and the Reconstruction Finance Corporation had more substance, with roots dating back many years. Essentially, the RFC, once a depression-fighting agency, had been allowed to survive into an era when it was not needed, and when its loans were often obtained for dubious enterprises—by dubious means. The Internal Revenue situation was largely a product of the sudden enormous rise in business profits and taxes, with consequent strong temptation toward tax evasion through connivance on the part of local tax collectors. Many of these latter went to jail, along with several medium-level bureaucrats from the Treasury and Justice Departments in Washington.

No President enjoys scandals, and Truman's native pugnacity was aroused by the attention which a hostile press accorded those of his administration. He stoutly denied, in office and afterward, that anything very bad had happened. What the Republicans jubilantly called "the mess in Washington," Truman contemptuously dismissed as "flyspecks."

If Truman's characterization of the scandals was a bit cavalier, nevertheless the view across the years suggests that their importance was once exaggerated. Harry Vaughan was no Harry M. Daugherty, and even the RFC investigation, which brought prominence to Senator J. William Fulbright of Arkansas, no Teapot Dome.

In any case, the crookedness of a number of big and small bureaucrats— very few of whom had more than a remote connection with Harry Truman —should not distort the focus on the Truman administration's landmark achievements. Two momentous successes by the army of nuclear physicists and other scientists who had now become a regular part of the government's labor force trace to Truman's forward-looking decisions on national atomic

1952: Truman's hand-picked candidate. Adlai Stevenson, the "egghead" Governor of Illinois, reluctantly accepted the Democratic party's nomination for President in Chicago's International Amphitheater. Here President Truman, who had first asked Stevenson to run in January 1952, tells the delegates, "This is the man!"

Truman was cordial in spite of a rough campaign, and worked hard to insure a smooth transition of administrations. Here he and President-elect Eisenhower exchange a smile and a handshake before leaving for the inauguration. Later that day Mr. Truman and his family were surprised with a sentimental farewell party at the home of Dean Acheson in Georgetown, after which they left by train for Independence, Missouri.

policy. The world's first atomic-powered submarine, the *Nautilus,* destined to carry out a historic reconnaissance under the North Pole, was launched, and the world's first thermonuclear explosion was set off at Eniwetok Atoll in the Pacific.

The failure forecast by Stimson to get international agreement for the control of atomic energy made the new developments seem more ominous than promising. But one has only to imagine the effect on Congress, press and public of the news that Russia had exploded an H-bomb and launched a nuclear submarine ahead of the U.S. to perceive the wisdom of Truman's course in pushing atomic development at full speed. One of his principal contributions was the approval of the testing facility at Yucca Flats, Nevada. There was a widespread belief that the American people, while wanting to keep the country's lead in atomic energy, would not sit still for "shooting off A-bombs" inside the U.S. Truman asked Gordon Dean, head of the Atomic Energy Commission, two questions: Would a continental U.S. testing ground really speed up the atomic-weapons program, and could it be surrounded by strong guarantees against anybody getting hurt? By the end of 1952 twenty atomic explosions had been carried out.

The majority of newspaper editors and radio-TV commentators preferred talking about Harry Vaughan and the scandals to discussing the implications of the atomic testing program—some of which at least were constructive and hopeful. The nation had put $7,000,000,000 into nuclear energy research and development. Results of tremendous significance were foreshadowed in medicine, biology, agriculture, and many other fields.

An important minor achievement of the Truman administration received less credit than it should have. In 1947 Truman stirred a teapot tempest in Congress and the press by adding a balcony to the south portico of the White House. To most people the White House was something sacred that nobody should touch, though practically every President has made alterations. But the next year Truman, who knew something about buildings, discovered that the whole structure was dangerously near collapse. The Truman family moved across the street to Blair House, normally reserved for official guests, while the entire interior of the White House was removed. Utmost care was taken with historic furnishings, the outer walls were underpinned with concrete, and a steel skeleton erected inside. When the three-year job was finished visitors discovered a subtly transformed mansion, the old mixture of rococo-and-random replaced by a homogeneous décor of graceful elegance. Few serious changes have been made in the White House since, and few are likely to be for some time to come. (Contrary to what many people imagine, the Kennedys made no substantial alterations.)

But as the second Truman administration drew to a close, the overblown issues of scandals and Communism in government occupied far more space in the newspapers and time on the air than did the solid achievements. Four more years added strength to the 1948 feeling that the Democrats had been in too long. Finally, the Democrats' 1948 will-o'-the-wisp, Dwight D. Eisenhower, turned into the Republicans' 1952 white hope.

Truman personally hand-picked the Democratic candidate, the brilliant, introspective, eloquent, and unwilling Governor of Illinois, Adlai E. Stevenson. Stevenson ran a fine race, but despite a record Democratic vote of over 27,000,000, Eisenhower won easily, with an incredible total of 34,000,000 votes. It was a resounding triumph for the popular general, but less so for the Republican party, which scored only a narrow coattail victory in the congressional races.

Notwithstanding friction over Stevenson's reluctance to run, which at least equaled Truman's in 1944, the sixty-eight-year-old President gave the Democratic ticket strong support. A memorable moment of the campaign came in Boston. Senator McCarthy, who was indulging his talent for unrestrained invective, had vilified General Marshall as a traitor. Eisenhower, an old comrade-in-arms and wartime subordinate of Marshall, was left in an embarrassing position. Truman addressed a Boston rally of hard-core Democratic partisans. He told them what McCarthy had said about Marshall, and accused Eisenhower of failing to come to Marshall's defense. Then, sticking out his chin, he said: *"I stand by my friends."* It was language Democrats understood in Boston as in Missouri, and it brought down the house.

Despite a few abrasions from the campaign, Truman and Eisenhower managed to organize an efficient transition of administrations. The atmosphere at the inaugural ceremonies, however, was chilly, with Eisenhower refusing a Truman luncheon invitation. Instead the Trumans went to lunch at the Achesons'.

En route Margaret suddenly turned around and said, "Hello, *Mr.* Truman!" Mr. Truman, who had been Judge, Senator, Vice-President and President throughout Margaret's entire life, broke into a roar of laughter.

At Washington's Union Station the old presidential car they had used for the famous whistlestop campaign was waiting to carry the Trumans home

In traditional robes of an Oxford don, the former President received an honorary degree of Doctor of Civil Law from the famous British university in 1956. Before the ceremonies, Mr. Truman strolled around the Oxford campus with Chancellor Alick Smith.

The morning walk. In Chicago, during the 1956 Democratic Convention, Mr. Truman toured Michigan Avenue at his usual brisk pace, supplying copy for newsmen as he went.

Margaret Truman became Mrs. Clifton Daniel, Jr., April 21, 1956, in the same Independence church where her parents were married thirty-seven years before. BELOW, Margaret arrived in Independence several days before the wedding and was greeted at the railroad station by her happy parents.

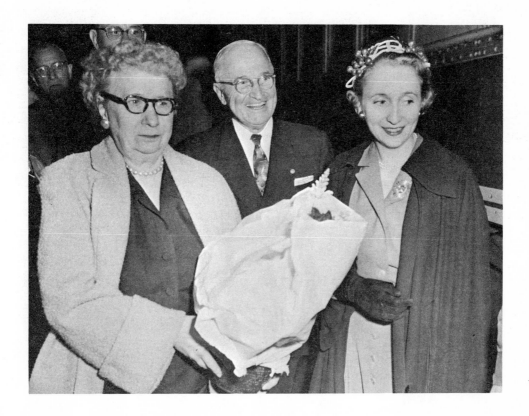

to Independence. They were surprised to find that some nine thousand people had deserted the inauguration parade to come say goodby. It was a sentimental occasion, with many eyes filled with tears, and with Harry Truman's face smeared with lipstick. He made his last speech from the back platform. The train pulled out, someone inevitably started "Auld Lang Syne" and the station rafters were set ringing.

The Latin poet Juvenal summed up what a wise man might reasonably expect from Heaven in the phrase, "A sound mind in a sound body." An idea that has long appealed to Americans, it was well illustrated by a familiar image of the 1950s and 1960s—former President Harry Truman on his early-morning walk, trailed by reporters who were having difficulty keeping up with his brisk pace and at the same time scribbling down his pungent answers to their questions.

The 6 A.M. constitutional was a Truman trademark from the time the farm boy moved to the city. "There's nobody around to bother you at six A.M.," he explained. This remained true in Independence, "where people are used to me," even when it ceased to be so in New York, Chicago, and Los Angeles. Sometimes in the big city an early morning cab driver pulled up and called out, "When are you going to ride again, Harry?"

Turning down all offers of million-dollar salaries to pose as head of a giant corporation, the former President devoted himself to his own pet project, the Truman Library in Independence. But he found time for something else he had always wanted to do—talk to America's young people. He accepted as many invitations as he possibly could to visit schools and colleges. Invariably his talk was followed by a lively Q & A—which was the part Truman liked best.

A student asked about the "Give 'em hell, Harry!" which he had so often heard from audiences. Truman: "I have never deliberately given anybody hell. I just tell the truth on the opposition—and they think it's hell."

"Isn't money getting to be too important in securing nominations and elections?" another asked. Truman did not think money had to be the deciding element. "I never had enough money to run a campaign in my county where I first held public office. I never had enough money to run a campaign for the presidency in 1948. Yet we won."

What does it take then to win an election? "It takes a candidate who understands what the people want. That's worth more than all the money he may be able to put together."

A student asked if he considered the Constitution "a conservative or a liberal document?" Truman: "It is both. It depends on the interpretation. It took the Court a long time to find those words in the Constitution which made it a liberal document. On the other hand, throughout our history, there were some Justices who took the view that the Constitution was written for the benefit of special privilege. But by trial and experience we managed to find out what was right for the country. And that's the way it should be. You couldn't have had this freedom of interpretation if you had somebody whose final word is law."

One student had read that some members of the Roosevelt administration "did not take too kindly to you at first when you became President." Truman readily acknowledged it. "I took little notice because I understood exactly how people who were close to Roosevelt felt . . . They were probably afraid that the country would go to the dogs with a new man who they thought didn't know much about what to do . . . I never held a grudge against any of them, not even those who were indiscreet enough to voice their misgivings or disapproval of me publicly."

He relished questions on the history of the presidency, on which he was an expert. Washington, Jefferson, Jackson, and Lincoln were among the greatest, Andrew Johnson one of the least appreciated, Generals Taylor and Grant among the least successful, Chester A. Arthur, a sort of "Republican Tammany politician," a very good President except that "he sold all the fine furniture that Jefferson, Adams and Monroe had brought over from France to furnish the White House. He sold nine van loads of White House furniture at auction for nine thousand dollars."

In 1964 Mr. Truman was guest of honor at Westminster College in Fulton, Missouri, where eighteen years earlier he had introduced Winston Churchill for the Iron Curtain speech. Westminster was breaking ground for the Winston Churchill Memorial and Library.

Now eighty, Truman regaled the audience with the story of the railroad journey across the country: "Something happened to cause a game of chance to take place . . . He said, 'Harry, does a pair of tens beat a pair of knaves?' He had a ten showing, I had a 'knave' showing. I said, 'You just try to make

Visitors to the Truman Library in Independence received warm welcomes from the former President. In 1959 Senator John F. Kennedy came to call. and in 1961 former President Eisenhower. President Johnson spoke at the Truman Library January 20, 1966, during ceremonies announcing the establishment of the Harry S Truman Center for the Advancement of Peace. Seated behind the President are Chief Justice Earl Warren, Mr. Truman, and Mrs. Truman. President Johnson also came to Independence in 1966 to sign the Medicare bill, for which Truman had fought.

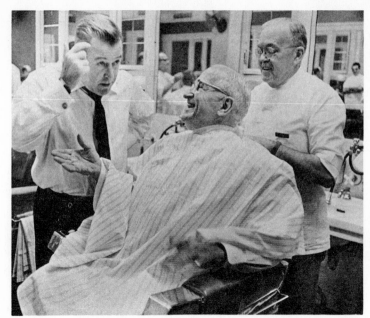

Time out for a haircut came in Seattle during a hectic campaign trip to the Far West for the Democratic ticket in 1960. Senator Warren Magnuson of Washington traded quips with the former President, who had the satisfaction of helping John F. Kennedy win a close race.

Doting grandfather Truman and his two Daniel grandsons, Clifton, center, and William Wallace, in 1962 at the Hotel Carlyle in New York City.

it work.' He turned over his pair of tens. But I didn't have the other jack.
It cost him a dollar to find out . . ."

In addition to the library in Independence, another building project close
to Truman's heart was rising in 1967–68 a long way from Missouri. The
Harry S Truman Center for the Advancement of Peace, on Mount Scopus
overlooking the Garden of Gethsemane in Jerusalem, was designed to help
Arabs, Jews, and all the people of the troubled Near East come together
and work for peace. At eighty-three he gave peace a sober appraisal: "We
must learn to abolish war lest war abolish us."

With the passage of time, historians take over from newspapermen. Emphasis shifts. Once trumpeted problems slip to the status of footnotes. The
real question in regard to the Truman administration, modern historians
feel, is whether it overestimated the expansionist ambitions of Soviet Russia
and thereby intensified the Cold War.

Henry Wallace may have been a little righter than Harry Truman thought,
though in the absence of Soviet documents (not to mention American),
that promises to be an open question for some time to come. It must be
remembered in any case that Truman did not invent his suspicions of Stalin.
In the eyes of the overwhelming majority of Americans they were so well
justified that it is difficult to conceive of an American President pursuing
a more conciliatory policy toward Moscow than Truman did. On the contrary, it is easy to picture an American President pursuing a much much
more truculent policy, perhaps with catastrophic results. In the context of
the 1940s, when Communism appeared to be a united, pervasive menace,
Truman showed a sensible restraint in dealing with it. He exhibited a healthy
skepticism toward congressional Red-baiting, above all that of the sinister
Senator McCarthy.

Up against the hardest, most unpopular decision a President of the United
States ever had to make, he fired a Hollywood-handsome, newspaper-heroic
general rather than let the country slide into a war that might have engulfed
the world in flames. At that moment, Harry Truman may have been
America—plain, everyday, democratic-with-a-small-D America—at its best.

Of the decisions, reactions, and creations that went to meet the storm
flow of problems, domestic and foreign, of 1945–52, much remains in con-
troversial abeyance. Many of the primary sources are still classified, and
scholars have hardly begun to work. But on the basis of what is known, it

may be said that Truman left a threefold heritage which has become part of the American governmental policy and purpose:

First, the Fair Deal idea—not a New Deal emergency reform, but a never-ending advance toward more and more welfare for more and more people. The American Medical Association characterized Truman's Medicare proposal as "European social democracy." Finally signed into law by President Johnson—in the Truman Library in Independence, with its original sponsor a smiling witness—Medicare is surely a piece of American social democracy. That there is much more to come few can doubt.

Second, the Truman Doctrine idea of limited response to aggression. Much sarcasm was expended when Truman described the Korean war as a "police action." But the police-action concept prevented a Communist blunder from blowing up into a world war, and provided a pattern that future Presidents would ignore at their peril.

Finally, the "Point Four" idea. Continuing assistance, technical as well as financial, tailored to the needs of each developing country, remains the cornerstone of long-range American foreign policy.

Samuel Eliot Morison, in his *Oxford History of the American People,* (1965) gives Truman extremely high marks: "Harry S Truman . . . was an inconspicuous-looking President, but one of the most conspicuously successful. Few statesmen have profited as much from history . . . President Truman's native intelligence enabled him to grasp quickly the situation into which he was so suddenly thrown, and on which he had not been briefed by Roosevelt . . . He won the friendship and respect of gentlemen in politics, such as Dean Acheson, soldiers such as General Marshall, and foreign statesmen such as Clement Attlee. He made good cabinet, judicial and ambassadorial appointments; he kept a firm hand on the new department of defense and the foreign service; and with more fateful decisions than almost any President in our time, he made the fewest mistakes."

Truman himself was more modest in his claim. He asked only that Americans remember him in the terms of his favorite epitaph, which he saw in Tombstone, Arizona:

HERE LIES JACK WILLIAMS · HE DONE

HIS DAMNEDEST

THE TRUMAN CABINET

The first name given is a holdover from the Roosevelt administration, except in the case of the Secretary of Defense, whose post was created by the unification of the armed forces in 1947.

Secretary of State: Edward R. Stettinius, Jr. (1944–45); James F. Byrnes (1945–47); George C. Marshall (1947–49); Dean G. Acheson (1949–53).

Secretary of the Treasury: Henry Morgenthau, Jr. (1934–45); Fred M. Vinson (1945–46); John W. Snyder (1946–53).

Secretary of War: Henry L. Stimson (1940–45); Robert P. Patterson (1945–47); Kenneth C. Royall (1947).

Secretary of the Navy: James V. Forrestal (1944–47).

Secretary of Defense: James V. Forrestal (1947–49); Louis A. Johnson (1949–50); George C. Marshall (1950–51); Robert A. Lovett (1951–53).

Attorney General: Francis Biddle (1941–45); Tom C. Clark (1945–49); J. Howard McGrath (1949–52); James P. McGranery (1952–53).

Postmaster General: Frank C. Walker (1940–45); Robert E. Hannegan (1945–47); Jesse M. Donaldson (1947–53).

Secretary of the Interior: Harold L. Ickes (1933–46); Julius A. Krug (1946–49); Oscar L. Chapman (1949–53).

Secretary of Agriculture: Claude R. Wickard (1940–45); Clinton P. Anderson (1945–48); Charles F. Brannan (1948–53).

Secretary of Commerce: Henry A. Wallace (1945–46); W. Averell Harriman (1946–48); Charles Sawyer (1948–53).

Secretary of Labor: Frances Perkins (1933–45); Lewis B. Schwellenbach (1945–48); Maurice J. Tobin (1948–53).

Silhouetted against the rising sun, Harry Truman crosses the street during his morning walk in Independence. Back in his home town, the former President's daily walks and other activities got little notice. He liked it that way.

INDEX

A NOTE ABOUT THIS BOOK

The text is set in *Times Roman* linotype, a version of the original *Times New Roman* designed by the late Stanley Morrison. Title page and chapter headings are set in *Perpetua,* designed by Eric Gill. Typography and binding were designed by Joseph P. Ascherl.